Cockney Dialect
and Slang

Cockney Dialect and Slang

PETER WRIGHT

B.T. BATSFORD LTD · LONDON

To the fork an' knife
(never a trouble an' strife)
and the Gawd forbids

First published 1981
Reprinted 1981
© Peter Wright 1981
ISBN 0 7134 2242 4
Phototypeset in Monophoto Baskerville by
Servis Filmsetting Ltd, Manchester
Printed in Great Britain by
Billing & Sons Ltd, London, Guildford and Worcester
for the publishers B.T. Batsford Ltd,
4 Fitzhardinge Street, London W1H 0AH

Contents

6

Acknowledgments

At cruxes of the survey I was greatly helped by the staff of the Guildhall Library and the Montefiori Community Education Centre in Stepney. There are many informants to whom through the years I have been greatly indebted, one being Jack Dash, the retired dockers' leader, who was of tremendous assistance. Others who answered recent enquiries most knowledgeably and enthusiastically included: Miss Isabel Barker of Stepney, Miss Rose Benson of Bethnal Green, Mrs Violet Cadden and Mrs Dolly Clarke of Stepney, Mr W.T. Cooling of Bethnal Green, Mr H.W. Dolphin of Poplar, Mrs W. Falco of Northolt, Mr G. Hames of Millwall, Miss Sarah Peck of Bethnal Green, Mr J. Rogers of Bermondsey, Mr and Mrs S. Silverman of Whitechapel, the Rev. Eddie Stride of Whitechapel, Mrs C. Trenell of Wapping, Mrs Annie Wenman of Stepney and Mr N. Wright of Deptford.

To these and all others involved in the searches I am most grateful.

Introduction

The chief reason for this book is to make Cockney much better known. So it should be, for it is the speech of *Lunnon Tahn* which, despite its old homely name, is not only a city but among the most important in the world.

Excellent works have appeared on certain aspects of Cockney. Its rhyming slang has been the subject of several most entertaining books; Eva Sivertsen has written in careful detail about its sounds; there is Matthews' scholarly and comprehensive *Cockney Past and Present*, although it actually refers to little later than pre-war Cockney.

By contrast, *Cockney Dialect and Slang* is a wide-ranging analysis of Cockney up to and into the 1980s. It treats vocabulary of all kinds (straightforward words, dialect, ordinary slang, rhyming and other special forms of slang) because this is what has always fascinated most people. Moreover, besides pronunciation it deals with Cockney grammar, a little-researched subject but one that is very necessary to show the dialect in action as a living thing, not a mere language corpse or collection of dead isolated words.

It is hoped that the book will stimulate and instruct not only teachers and students, but all who, whilst not being specialists, have a lively and intelligent interest in language.

Does London really have a dialect? To investigate this I was specially sent around the metropolis in 1952 as first fieldworker for the well-known Leeds University Survey of English Dialects under Professor H. Orton because his co-director of the Survey, the eminent Swiss dialectologist Professor Eugen Dieth, doubted whether any Cockney remained. Strange as it may seem, other language experts had been in some doubt; for Joseph Wright's London examples in his classic *English Dialect Dictionary* are rare and seem at times almost casually inserted, whilst A.J. Ellis,[1] though himself brought up in North London, makes the surprising statement that 'all London north of the Thames . . . is essentially a place where dialect could not grow up because of the large mass of changing and more or less educated population'. How pleased, therefore, Professor Dieth was when my London recordings refuted the theory that its dialect was dead.

I still have vivid personal recollections of those days – for example, of accommodation provided in one London district by Toc H and in another unofficially (but, let it be stressed, morally correctly) by a helpful barmaid. There was the meeting with the good dialect speaker who was also an inventor and who was at great pains to explain his curious inventions prominent in his back garden. There was the startling incident in some almshouses in *Sahf 'Ackney* when my tape-recorder, innocently plugged into direct current, blew up. But regardless of obstacles the work smoothly proceeded.

A further important question is whether the Thames cuts traditional London speech into recognisable halves. In 1890 Ellis[2] suggested that this was probably true and in 1910 it was claimed by MacBride[3] 'The London dialect is really, especially on the South side of the Thames, a perfectly legitimate and responsible child of the old Kentish tongue. . . . The dialect of London north of the Thames has been shown to be one of the many varieties of the Midland or Mercian dialect, flavoured by the East Anglian variety of the same speech, owing to the great influx of Essex people into London'. Quite recently, though much more guardedly,[4] it has been stated, '"Genuine" Cockney is supposed to have two principal geographical varieties, centred on the foci of the East End and Walworth-Bermondsey-Southwark respectively'. Yet countless masses of Londoners cross the Thames daily by train, car and on foot and great rivers like the Thames, provided they are crossable, have been meeting-points of dialects and communication, not barriers.

In 1952 five places were systematically recorded in the London area. Since some 1800 unloaded questions were asked in each place, and since by that time I had been a full-time fieldworker for three years and the results were checked and re-checked by a most able team, they are supposed to be the most accurate and comprehensive then available. They cannot show everything; but they do indicate traditional speech, especially of the elderly, in five widely scattered parts of Greater London, namely *Sahf 'Ackney* in the East End, *Ahminsworth* 'Harmondsworth' in the old county of Middlesex, Nettleswell in Essex, Walton-on-the-Hill in Surrey and

Farningham in Kent. The farthest distances between these places
are about 35 miles north to south and 32 miles east to west. Their
results are to my mind surprisingly homogeneous, although they
do illustrate as Ellis suggested a slightly more southern dialect
background south of the Thames.

Of course investigations have not stopped there, and since then I
have made many dialect hunts in the London area, e.g. for many
years when examining duties took me regularly to London on
behalf of Cambridge and London Universities. Moreover in recent
years I have been adding to this knowledge as part of an
investigation into the language of other British cities.

How to write Cockney in such a book as this has always been a
problem. In 1915 Alfred Anscombe[5] found it so: 'Well fust aout
there's the spellin, which ees muyty differcult. Cause why? Cause
we aighn't gaut letters enough. See ere naow. Few've any desuyer
ter be c'rect down yew ivver spell the litery word "paper" wiv an i
in Cauckney – nawt unless yer hindulgin in carrerkertoor'.

The only thoroughly scientific way is to use phonetic symbols,
which is how I always record when on fieldwork; but for a book like
this it would be hopelessly off-putting. Therefore in these pages the
Cockney has been restricted to approximate spelling, though I
would be the first to agree with an informant's remark that 'As de
Cockney is writ, it ain't right'. Some variation has been allowed –
e.g. words like 'the' appear sometimes as *the*, sometimes as *de*, just as
happens in layers of the dialect. For ease of reading I have
normalised words like 'town', writing the most traditional Cockney type *tahn*; but have resisted the temptation to turn, e.g. every
'lady' into *lydy* and terms like 'boat race' into *bowt rice*, even though
their sounds do approach those spellings. The aim has been to
scrutinise Cockney without in the process making it unintelligible
for the general reader.

It is a shame that, whereas the dialects of many country villages
have been meticulously collected, that of London with its teeming
millions has been almost studiously ignored, chiefly it seems
because quaintness adds a glamour to rural dialects. People
sometimes tell me, 'London words are not so unusual'. Perhaps
not, but the purpose is to capture living speech, not the strangest
oddities fossilised in glossaries of London.

If you happen to speak a form of Cockney, you are part of a great
family and should be proud of it; if you are a 'half-breed' with

perhaps a London *mam* and a Yorkshire dad you should be quite interested, if only to suggest where I may be wrong (amendments and additions would be most welcome); whilst, whoever you are, it is hoped that the book can be easily understood, to give pleasure and much information about the speech of 'the world's finest city'.

I
Historical Background

What is Cockney?

A Cockney originally meant someone born and spending all his or her life in London, traditionally within the sound of Bow Bells – in other words, within about a quarter of a mile of the church of St Mary-le-Bow in Cheapside in east central London and not far from London Bridge, Billingsgate fish-market and the Mansion House. However, today this definition cannot literally be true as the district just round that church is not residential. At week-ends it is dead, and the nearest residential communities, around Whitechapel and the Golden Lane estate by the Barbican, would generally be out of earshot of such bell-ringing. Other accepted Cockney communities like those of Shoreditch, East Stepney, Bethnal Green and Hackney are still farther away.

Many Cockneys are still to be found in neighbourhoods such as Whitechapel, *Lime'ahs, Cannin' Tahn, Plarstow* (Plaistow), Islington and Wapping, which is famous for its Cockney dialect. But even this is far too strict a definition of Cockneyland, for it excludes natives of many other districts like Bermondsey, Lambeth, Millwall and Tottenham who would claim with good reason that they are typical Londoners.

Cockney is from Middle English *cokeney* 'cock's egg'. Originally it meant a small or misshapen egg and was probably a synonym for anything odd. It became a term of reproach and ridicule, meaning an effeminate silly person, probably first used by villagers living round the capital to describe the Londoners they met. Chaucer in his prologue to the *Reeve's Tale* used *cokeney* in connection with *daffe*, i.e. a fool.

For many years it seems to have remained mostly an unkind term. Pierce Egan, writing his *Life in London* in 1821, stated that

11

everyone knew Cockney to mean 'an uneducated native of London . . . pert and conceited, yet truly ignorant'. Over a century later, Professor H.C. Wyld in his *Universal English Dictionary* noted it for a townsman who was 'vulgar, presuming, trivial'. It is linked with the modern word *cocky* 'bumptious, conceited'. 'Don't call them Cockneys', I was warned by an East End vicar who works right in their midst. They do resent this term from mere goggling tourists, but in fact I found that many of his parishioners were proud of being Cockney, feeling that they were the real part of London.

Northerners could be expected to have a more jaundiced view of what a Cockney is. In *Ab o'th' Yate's* 1881 Lancashire dictionary he is called 'A man ut thinks hissel th'fust Englishman i'th'lond, but conno talk English. He coes everybody born eautside the seaund o' Big Ben a "bladdy caintryman"'

Cockney is now used rather vaguely for speech of the London area. It is generally applied to lower-class speech, 'London' referring to a more educated type. Julian Franklyn in *The Cockney* distinguishes between the 'light' Cockney of the Cockney clerk (i.e. that softened by years of formal education) and the 'deep' Cockney of the coster. This kind of comment is of course true with almost any dialect, that there are several layers from the broadest to the most refined. As for its geographical area, old East-Enders claim that 'Cockney' is spoken in Shoreditch, Bethnal Green, Stepney, Hackney and across the Thames in Bermondsey, and that overspill areas like Hainult (to which people have moved from inner London) are perhaps even more Cockney; but that other parts of London like New Cross and Peckham are outside the real bounds of Cockney. By this they mean 'broad Cockney'.

Cockney and Standard English

Ever since 1066, when William the Conqueror established London as the capital of England, Cockney has been easily the most important dialect influence on accepted English speech. Previously Winchester in King Alfred's ancient kingdom of Wessex had been the most influential centre for English speech, but now things changed radically.

Until at least 1350 London English had some Essex features (such as *e* from Old English *y*, once thought only a Kentish feature), but soon it veered more towards the dialects of Middlesex,

Hertfordshire and the South-East Midlands.

The crucial factor was the dramatic rise in importance of the City of London after the Norman Conquest as an administrative and ecclesiastical centre (before then it had been little more than the capital of Essex). This growth naturally attracted more and more people. For 300 years French and Latin had great influence on the languages of church and state, but English was always the speech of the ordinary Londoner. When in the fourteenth century Norman influence began to decline, that of London English grew; and at this vital time, as population records show, most newcomers to London were arriving from Bedfordshire, Huntingdonshire and Northamptonshire in the South-East Midlands.

This provided the mixture out of which in the next hundred years grew the London English which was not Standard English but which provided the base from which modern Standard English later evolved. Chaucer had used the dialect spoken in London for his prose and poetry, Hoccleve used it too, but the new London speech was different. An upper-class dialect developed in London in the fourteenth and fifteenth centuries mainly from these settlers from the East Midlands, and in the sixteenth century Puttenham stated that a difference was recognised between upper-class English and that of the humbler classes.

London dialect attained greater prestige simply because it was used more frequently than any other. Speakers of other dialects became aware that, to gain acceptance in the capital, they would have to modify their accents towards that of London. By 1700, variations in writing Standard English had almost gone. The development of print, which could 'freeze' the standard, ensured that highly educated London English became accepted as the ideal. This is still its position some 500 years later, and the standard is reinforced every time Londoners watch television, listen to the radio or pick up a newspaper. This, then, is how Standard English emerged; but only to a fairly small degree has it been at the direct expense of Cockney.

Older Cockney writings

Henry Machyn's diary, which he wrote from 1550 to 1563, is not only the most informative, but also the most entertaining of the writings of early Cockney. In drama, Beaumont and Fletcher's *Knight of the Burning Pestle* is a most careful study of Cockney speech

of the time, George the grocer and Nell his wife being outstanding
for their delightful Cockney idiom.

Shakespeare's Doll Tearsheet in Henry IV is one Cockney
character, but his treatment of the Cockney is best seen there in
Mistress Quickly, 'hostess of a tavern in Eastcheap'. In pronunciation her most marked Cockney trait is the first vowel of *exion*
'action'. Otherwise her dialect characteristics are much more
general ones like *ay* 'yes', *afore* 'before', *swounded* 'swooned', *shaked*
'shaken' and *a thousand pound*. Like a modern Cockney in awe of
long unknown words who talks, say of *'eavititis* for hepatitis, so Mrs
Quickly utters malapropisms like *canaries* for quandaries and
Ginny's Case for genitive case. It is not unlikely that on
Shakespeare's stage at the Globe Theatre near the south bank of
the Thames, most of his low-life characters were played as
Cockneys even when the setting was abroad in Rome, Messina, etc.
The commoners at the start of *Julius Caesar* pun like those in his
London plays, whilst the mechanics in *Midsummer Night's Dream*
and Dogberry and Verges in *Much Ado* seem quite English.

Samuel Foote, the actor and dramatist, was one of the first
writers to formalise the Cockney. In *The Mayor of Garratt*, 1764,
through the speech of his City penmaker Jerry Sneak, particularly
his confusions of *w* and *v*, he founded a famous line of Cockneys in
literature, of which Dickens's Sam Weller (in *Pickwick Papers*) and
Mrs Gamp (in *Martin Chuzzlewit*) along with Thackeray's Jeames
Yellowplush are the outstanding examples.

At the summit of older Cockney writers stands Charles Dickens.
One house (now open as a museum) where he did much of his
writing is in Doughty Street, a little east of London University and
only about a mile from the heart of traditional Cockneyland. He
used to enjoy tramping miles through London (and going on
expeditions to other parts of England) mostly to gather the
language and atmosphere, and partly as a welcome break from his
family. From his years spent reporting in the House of Commons
and his untiring efforts to listen to and question people first-hand,
his command of Cockney idiom was certain. *Sketches by Boz* (1836),
for example, illustrates it admirably. Linguistically important in
Pickwick Papers is his Cockney character Sam Weller who is notable
for his *v* for *w* (*ven* 'when', *visperin* 'whispering', etc.) besides the
opposite change as in 'you must be wery (very) fond o' cats'.

Mrs Gamp's speech includes many forms used by other characters in Dickens's novels, such being: (in pronunciation) *widder* 'widow', *nater* 'nature', *nothink* 'nothing', *wunst* 'once', *arterwards* 'afterwards'; (in word-endings) *you earns, you know'd, to have wrote*; (in syntax) *in course* 'of course', which may sound curious to modern ears but occurs frequently in the writings of Mayhew.

Occasionally Dickens allows masculine and feminine pronouns to refer to inanimate objects. In *Our Mutual Friend* Mrs Boffin declares of a book 'Bought him at a sale' and Mr Venus predicts of a kettle 'She'll bile in a couple of minutes'. This type of speech is still current among very elderly natives of e.g. Exeter, though kettles there are usually masculine.

Dickens employs many words which are now out-of-date. To this class belong e.g. *wipe* 'pocket handkerchief' and *fogle* 'silk handkerchief' stolen by a *fogle-hunter* 'pickpocket'; *askings* 'publication of the banns of marriage'; and a goodly number of now-forgotten occupational terms such as *cad* 'bus conductor' (present-day ones would object to that name!), *chummy* 'chimney sweep', *jockey* 'clerk, office-boy', and *joskin* 'carter'. On the other hand, many of his lower-class terms live on, like *grub* 'food', *quod* 'prison' and *rheumatiks*. The whole subject is carefully treated in G.L. Brook's *Language of Dickens*, where he selects the following from Jo, the crossing-sweeper in *Bleak House*, as typical of the most sub-standard Cockney speech:

> 'They're wot's left, Mr Snagsby', says Joe, 'out of a sov'ring as was give me by a lady in a wale as sed she was a servant and as come to my crossin one night and asked to be showd this 'ere ouse and the ouse wot him as you giv the writin to died at, and the berrin-ground wot he's berrid in. She ses to me, she ses, "are you the boy at the Inkwhich?" she ses. I ses, "yes", I ses. She ses to me, she ses, "can you show me all them places?" And she ses to me "do it", and I dun it, and she give me a sov'ring and hooked it.'

Renton Nicholson, a contemporary of the young Charles Dickens, wrote *Cockney Adventures* which appeared in 1837–8. He had a fine command of Cockney idiom and slang. In sounds, it is noteworthy that he retained *v* for *w* as in a 'chap as vas along with (who was with) us', 'ven he com'd (when he came)'. Thackeray's 1840 burlesque *The Yellowplush Papers* is a rich store of Cockney, with convincing dialect spellings like *nothink* 'nothing' and *ax* 'ask'.

Finally among old Cockney writers we are bound to consider Henry Mayhew's great sociological work of 1851 onwards, *London Labour and the London Poor*. Its great value is that instead of giving masses of barely digestible statistics, he usually got Londoners to reveal conditions by telling their own stories which he reproduces in their own words. He sympathetically examines the life and work of the London costermongers, beggars, tramps and criminals; and his account is an invaluable fund of Cockney as spoken round about the 1840s. Typical are these replies of a 16-year-old coster boy[6]:

'There was two on us at home with mother . . . we was shocking hard up, and she pawned nigh everything. Sometimes, when we hadn't no grub at all, the other lads, perhaps, would give us some of their bread and butter . . . when it was dark we would go and lie down on the bed and try and sleep until she came home with the food. I was eight year old then.

'A man as know'd mother said to her, "Your boy's got nothing to do, let him come along with me and yarn a few ha'pence", and so I became a coster. . . . By using up the stock as we couldn't sell, we used to manage pretty tidy. When I was fourteen I took up with a girl. I used to walk out of a night with her and give her half pints of beer at the publics. She were about thirteen, and used to dress werry nice, though she wasn't above middling pretty. . . .

'On a Sunday I goes out selling, and all I yarns I keeps. Plays ain't in my line much; I'd sooner go to a dance – it's more livelier. The "penny gaffs" is rather more in my style; the songs are out and out, and makes our gals laugh. . . . If we lads ever has a quarrel, why, we fights for it. If I was to let a cove off once, he's do it again. If a cove was to fetch me a lick of the head, I'd give it him again, whether he was a big 'un or a little 'un. I'd precious soon see a henemy of mine shot afore I'd forgive him. . . . I never heerd about this here creation you speaks about. In coorse (of course) God Almighty made the world and the poor bricklayers' labourers built the houses arterwards . . . the gals the lads goes and lives with thinks with our walloping 'em werry cruel of us, but we don't. "Forgive us our trespasses", it's a very good thing, but no costers can't do it.'

Later Cockney

Now written Cockney begins to be presented differently. About 1876 the periodical *Punch* published a series of Cockney letters by F. Anstey which achieved a considerable reputation (for example, George Bernard Shaw referred to them). They appeared in print as the rhyming letters written by 'Arry to his pal Charlie. In them the slang vocabulary is strengthened by the addition of Americanisms, and significantly *w* no longer interchanges with *v*. In about 1880 James Greenwood brought out *Journeys through London*, which were sketches of London life and scenes taken from direct observation. He also is dubious about *v* and *w*, transposing them only on rare occasions.

The first writer to make wide use of the new type of Cockney dialect was A.W. Tuer in *The Kawkneigh Awlminek* 'Cockney Almanac' of 1883. In this work he formally buries the outstanding feature of older written Cockney with the remark 'Beware of the viddy (Beware of the widow) Samivel, my boy, beware of the widdy'. You will remember that Samuel Weller in Dickens's *Pickwick Papers* was exceptionally fond of *v* for *w*. Then in 1901 Barry Pain in the Tomkins verses of *The Daily Chronicle* adopted Tuer's newer style of written Cockney and developed it.

As Matthews reminds us, most authors whose work involved using Cockney dialogue adopted the new manner – Edwin W. Pugh in *A Street in London*, 1895; Somerset Maugham in *Liza of Lambeth*, 1897; Pett Ridge in *Mord Em'ly* 1898; Richard Whiteing in *No. 5 John St.*, 1899; Clarence Rook in *The Hooligan Nights*, 1899; A. Neil Lyons in *Hookey* and later stories. Since that time the Cockney literary convention that was settled in the 1880s has remained more or less unchanged.

The uneducated London English of H.G. Wells's novels sounds genuine enough. Take, for instance from 1902 these stray remarks of one of his heroes, Kipps, who to some extent is autobiographical: 'I can't get it orf nohow (off at all) . . . I done (did) it . . . went to a norfis (an office) . . . run froo (ran through) it . . . worf free (worth three) 'undred . . . I arst (asked) about it . . . Ann don't (doesn't) seem to fency (fancy) a moty- (motor-) car . . . lorst (lost) it all and gorn (gone)'.

The 'night-watchman' short stories of W.W. Jacobs are wonderful examples of Cockney humour. Here is an extract from one called 'An Odd Freak':

'Speaking o' money', said the night-watchman thoughtfully, as he selected an empty soap-box on the wharf for a seat, 'the whole world would be different if we all 'ad more of it. It would be a brighter and a 'appier place for everybody'.

'In about a week arter we was paid off at the Albert Docks these chaps was all cleaned out, and they was all in despair, with a thirst wot wasn't half quenched and a spree wot was on'y in a manner o' speaking just begun, and at the end of that time they came round to a room wot I 'ad, to see wot could be done. There was four of them in all: old Sam Small, Ginger Dick, Peter Russet, and a orphan nevy of Sam's . . . .

'Wot's the idea, Ginger?' says Sam, getting up to lend me and Russet a 'and with 'is nevy.

'My idea is this', ses Ginger: 'take 'is cloes off 'im and dress 'im up in that there winder-blind, or something o' the kind; tie 'im up with a bit o' line, and take 'im round to Ted Reddish in the 'Ighway and sell 'im for a 'undered quid as a wild man of Borneo'.

'You never saw anything like Beauty when they 'ad finished with 'im. If 'e was bad in 'is cloes, 'e was a perfeck horror without 'em. Ginger Dick faked 'im up beautiful, but there was no pleasing 'im. Fust 'e found fault with the winder-blind, which 'e said didn't fit; then 'e grumbles about going barefoot, then 'e wanted somethink to 'ide 'is legs, which was natural considering the shape of 'em.

'We must 'ave a cab', says old Sam.

'Cab?' ses Ginger. 'What for?'

'We should 'ave half Wapping following us', saye Sam.

. . . . the remarks of the cabman was eggstrordinary. 'e wouldn't start till 'e'd got double fare paid in advance; but they got in at last and drove off.

* * *

Ted Reddish cleared his throat. 'As the wild man wot you left on approval didn't seem to like 'Appy Cottage, we took 'im out an' put 'im in with the tiger'.

'Put 'im in with the *WOT?*' ses the unfort'nit man's uncle, jumping off 'is chair.

'The tiger', ses Reddish. 'We 'eard somethink in the night, but we thought they was only 'avin a little bit of a tiff, like. In the morning I went down with a bit o' cold meat for the wild man, and I thought at first he'd escaped; but looking a bit closer—'

'Don't, Ted', ses 'is wife. 'I can't bear it'. . . .

''Orrible', ses Sam 'uskily. 'You ought to ha' known better than to put 'im in with a tiger. Wot could you expect? W'y, it was a mad thing to do. . . . We want a 'undered quid off of you; an wot's more, we mean to 'ave it'.

'But the tiger's ate 'im', says Mrs Reddish, explaining.

'I know that', says Sam sharply. 'But 'e was our wild man, and we want to be paid for 'im. You should ha' been more careful. We'll give you five minutes; and if the money ain't paid by that time, we'll go straight off to the police station'.

For the outcome of this alarming story you should go back to the original in Jacobs.

One outstanding dramatist and portrayer of Cockney can never be forgotten – George Bernard Shaw. He was a far more accurate and original observer of the dialect even than he has been acclaimed, although he had to exaggerate it a little for stage purposes. He was, for instance, on the BBC committee for pronunciation. His own written attempts to record Cockney were as detailed as they could be without employing a phonetic alphabet, and he bequeathed a sum of money to devise a new alphabet of 40 symbols to cope with all the sounds of Standard English.

Shaw was a member of the Yorkshire Dialect Society, the oldest dialect society in the world, and modelled Professor Higgins of his 1920 play *Pygmalion* a good deal on another of its members, the distinguished phonetician Henry Sweet. This play, about the attempts to make Eliza Doolittle the Cockney flower-girl into a social success speaking impeccable Standard English, has captured the hearts and imaginations of many an audience, and has become world famous through its musical adaptation *My Fair Lady*. Professor Higgins wagers that he will pass off Eliza as an acceptable speaker of Standard English. His task is almost impossible, as can be seen from her language below where she is angrily telling his mother what she thinks of him:

There's menners f'yer! Te-oo banches o' voylets trod into the mad . . . . Ow eez yee-ooa san, is e? Well, fewd dan y'de-ooty bawmz a mother should, eed now bettern to spawl a pore gel's flahzn than ran awy athaht pyin. Will ye-oo py me f'them?
There's manners for you! Two bunches of violets trodden into the mud . . .
Oh, he's your son, is he? Well, if you'd done your duty by him as a mother

should, he'd know better than to spoil a poor girl's flowers and then run away without paying. Will you pay me for them?

What stands out again and again is that genuine interest in and knowledge of Cockney somehow shows through in a writer. Some writers, like Julian Franklin and George Bernard Shaw, have it. Others know it only second-hand, from books. To understand Cockney, a living language, do not simply read books about it, even the best ones. Listen to tape-recordings if you can, and best of all, if possible, listen to and talk face-to-face with Cockneys themselves, for they are the real experts.

Cockney in the music-hall

In music-hall songs Cockney has been very prominent. The old music-hall was a variety theatre presenting perhaps ten widely different acts per show under a master of ceremonies who took up his place before a lectern at the side of the stage (City Varieties just off the Headrow in Leeds is the oldest surviving British example; previously the oldest was one in Glasgow, now destroyed by fire). Unfortunately British music-halls are nearly extinct. In 1958 only four remained in London and by 1962 all of those had stopped showing variety programmes. Nevertheless for many years music-halls were the very life-blood of Cockney entertainment.

The music-halls popularised various catch-phrases, especially contemptuous or insulting ones like 'Put a sock in it (Stop it)!' and 'Keep yer 'air on (Stay calm)'.

About 1888 the Cockney charwoman first appeared on the music-hall stage in Henry Walker's ballad *Betsy Wareing* 'which (who) goes out a-chairing (*charring*, cleaning)'. They were the ancient forerunners of the Dais (Daisy) and Gert (Gertrude) sketches of the last war by Elsie and Doris Waters. The Cockney charwoman is noted for her gossip, which runs on and on, for example: 'Well, Gert, do you know? – 'e comes up to me an' 'e says, "Gert", 'e says, "Why did yer take that orf of mi plite (off my plate) . . . .".'

In 1891 Albert Chevalier took to the music-halls with instant success. He made his reputation by idealising the coster. His supreme gift was the ability to express deep affection and pathos, best expressed in *My Old Dutch*, the Cockney's familiar term for his wife, and ending with the chorus:

We've been togevver nah for forty year
An' it don't seem a day too much,
There ain't a lady livin' in the land
As I'd swop for mi dear ol' Dutch.

Contemporary with Chevalier were several great comedians who specialised in the songs of the *pearlies* (costermongers). Even today, processions of *pearly kings and queens* (costermongers and their women) are held in summer in London, the *pearlies* being so-called from their clothes adorned with pearl buttons. The tradition, which arose in the nineteenth century, may actually have been started by such comedians, who wore fanciful decorations as they sang costers' songs on the music-hall stage.

An artist who became very popular in the 1890s at the peak of the 'coster singer' craze was Gus Elen (1863–1940), whose best-known songs included 'Never Introduce Your Donah to a Pal', whose story and moral may be gathered from this verse:

Once I spotted Bill and Sal a-making eyes,
Then he goes and lushes (kisses) 'er, to my surprise,
I sez, 'Look 'ere, this is far beyond a joke',
He sez, 'Chuck it, else I'll land yer on the boke (head)'.
I spars up, but though yer won't believe the fact,
In one short round I gits my peepers (eyes) black'd,
From the cart Sal shouted, 'Gar'n, it sarves yer right',
In jumped Bill, and then the pair drew out o' sight.

We must remember that in such music-hall songs details of pronunciation were left to the artists. (It is just the same today when companies present the London musical *Oliver*). The published versions of their songs, written for a wider public, had standard spelling and so do not show Cockney sounds in detail.

The following is part of the most famous Cockney music-hall song. It gives opinions about the countryside of a London coster, someone about as far removed as possible from the effects of a rural existence. To make it sound like broad Cockney, ignoring the spelling you have to make *day* and *gay* sound respectively rather like *die* and *guy*, pronounce *'ouses* as *'ahses* and so on, just as the old singers would:

THE 'OUSES IN BETWEEN

If you saw my little backyard, 'What a pretty spot!' you'd cry
It's a picture on a summer day;
Wiv the turnip tops and cabbages what people don't buy
I makes it on a Sunday look all gay.
The neighbours fink I grows 'em, and you'd fancy you're in Kent,
Or at Epsom, if you gaze into the mews (stables)*;*
It's a wonder as the landlord doesn't want to raise the rent,
Because we've got such nobby (fine) *distant views.*

Chorus   *Oh! it is really a werry* (very) *pretty garden,*
            And Chingford to the eastward could be seen;
            Wiv (with) *a ladder and some glasses,*
            You could see to 'Ackney Marshes,
            If it wasn't for the 'ouses in between.

Though the gas-works isn't wiolets (aren't violets)*, they improve the rural scene –*
For mountains they would werry nicely pass;
There's the mushrooms in the dust-hole (cellar)*, with the cowcumbers* (cucumbers) *so green.*
It only wants (needs) *a bit o' 'ot-'ouse* (greenhouse) *glass.*
I wears this milkman's nightshire (smock)*, and I sits outside all day,*
Like the plough-boy cove (person) *what mizzled o'er the Lea* (disappeared across the River Lea, which runs through East London)*;*
And when I goes indoors at night they dunno (don't know) *what I say*
'Cause (because) *my language gets as yokel* (rustic) *as can be.*

Chorus   *Oh! it really is a werry pretty garden,*
            And the soap-works from the 'ouse-tops could be seen;
            If I got a rope and pulley,
            I'd enjoy the breeze more fully,
            If it wasn't for the 'ouses in between.

A feature of many broad-spoken Cockney men is claimed to be their loud voices and tendency to shout. This may well be true, as all inner London is so noisy. Harry Champion, an exponent of later music-hall songs like 'Ginger, you're Barmy (crazy)!' and 'Enery (Henry) the 8th I am', used to shout, and between his shouts could be plainly heard his great gulps for more breath. He also showed in 'Any Owd (old) Iron?', the call of the *totter* 'scrap-dealer', the

Cockney's perkiness and vitality; and in 'Boiled Beef and Carrots' his enormous love of eating. The harder Harry Champion shouted in his songs, the more his audiences loved it.

Although music-hall songs illustrate a variety of Cockney which is out-of-date, audiences would have felt cheated if what was being sung was just average or very mild in its amount of Cockney accent, Just as audiences listening to Northern comedians expect to hear *By Gum*!, so London music-hall audiences would be waiting for a *Cor Blimey*! (*Gum* and *Cor* being both corruptions of 'God'), even though other oaths such as *God*!, *'Struth*! (short for 'God's truth') and *Strike a light*! are more frequent. Similarly anywhere in the entertainment world an exaggerated Cockney accent now generally wins approval.

Recent and living Cockney

Recent Cockney entertainers have varied in style. A few like Harry Champion use a shouting, raucous approach. More of them, e.g. Max Miller, have been more subtle, emphasising Cockney wit and perkiness. The most popular now is fairly average, down-to-earth domestic Cockney, where what matters most to the audience is not the comicality of sounds but the general humour and the ideas.

On radio and television there are a good many situation comedies where characters use Cockney dialect for humorous purposes. One of the best known has been *Till Death us do Part* (a title taken from part of the marriage service), which is a comedy centred round the garrulous Alf Garnett and his family and set in East London. Episodes for the series were made in Wapping, and people are remembered there who were just like Alf. Here the dialect is quite genuine, with 'bloody', 'cup', 'rough', etc. pronounced almost with *a*-sounds, glottal stops in *bo'lle* 'bottle', etc., *f* and *v* respectively for voiceless and voiced *th* (*Smif* 'Smith', *anuvver* 'another'), and many *aints* and so forth. In this connection it is useful to read the autobiography of Johnny Speight (see Bibliography), who created Alf Garnett.

There is no shortage of Cockney speech-evidence. You can hear it from famous personalities being interviewed on radio and TV, such as Jack Dash, the old dockers' leader, and the boxer Henry Cooper. You can hear it from ordinary people. There is no need to rely on ancient Cockney writers – indeed that would be misleading. In the talk of famous personalities, newspaper articles, tape recordings and above all the speech that millions of Londoners are using every minute of every day, there are countless opportunities at various levels to hear and study Cockney.

2
General Vocabulary: Mainly About People

This chapter deals with Cockney words for people and what they say, but an explanation is first needed about the structure of Cockney vocabulary as a whole.

Language is a tool of society and people talk like those around them. To speak any other way would mark them off as strange. Therefore Cockneys talk like other Cockneys, not BBC announcers. They cannot talk back to the *wireless* or *telly* to 'improve their diction', and for their children a few hours a day in school is little compared with all the time spent with friends and relations.

The general composition of Cockneys' ordinary vocabulary is not so remarkable. Naturally there are some Scandinavian words, such as *leg* and *sky*; but fewer than in the North, where *becks*, *gills* and so forth abound because the Vikings did so much of their early raiding in those parts. French and Latin words are also easily met – *cul-de-sac* and *joke*, for example – but far fewer than in Standard English, for which it has been claimed[7] that our forefathers borrowed from French and Latin over 10,000 words before 1500 and a full quarter of the vocabulary of Latin.

Cockney takes words from almost every language in the world – *skipper* and *sketch*, for instance, from Dutch, that nation having been our greatest sea rivals and famous for its master-painters; *opera* and *spaghetti* from Italian; *potatoes* via Spanish; *sputnik* from Russian; *alkali* from Arabic, *zinc* from German, and so forth. Some are quite unusual borrowings, like *coggage* 'writing-paper' from Hindustani (from *kaghaz*, e.g. 'Where's de coggage?').

Others arrive from originally technical language, such as *biro* which now stands for any ball-point pen, and *hoover* for any such cleaning apparatus, not merely the products of the original firms. Still others approach Cockney through slang: *doodle-bug* would be an appropriate example, for the German V2 rockets that helped to devastate so much of the East End during the last war. Some words, like whistle and thump, imitate the sounds that Cockneys make and hear. Still others, like *bloke* (man) and *cock* (mate, friend), are of rather doubtful origin; whilst the history of others like *pig* is ultimately obscure.

Some general warnings

Beware of imagining that all the words explained in this book obey a rigid, never-to-be broken set of language rules. Words, not unlike families, have their ups-and-downs. They too rise and fall in the social scale. For a period Cockney will greatly favour a word, and then for no apparent reason want to *chuck it aht*. Slang words may be accepted, even become the height of fashion like *cab* or *bus*. Others may drop out of vogue when the thing they denote disappears, as happened to the wartime *black-out* (and even more rapidly to its journalistic shortening *blout*). Some words, such as *nice*, or *smashin'* in the sense of being very good, have no precise meaning at all. To an elderly Cockney the weather can be *nice*, and the food and a journey and the people around him; to a younger one a soccer game may be *smashin'*, and likewise a dress, a haircut and a pop-star, though nothing is actually broken. Such words have few shades of meaning.

A second warning is that words do not always mean what they seem to mean. To be asked, 'Know what time it is, mate?' does not merit the answer 'Indeed I can tell the time, my man', unless you want to risk being *done up* (attacked and beaten). Similarly 'Who's is this jacket?' or 'Who's left 'is car right in the drive?' can mean 'Move it at once'. The underlying meaning is taken for granted.

A third caution is that new words sometimes appear in Cockney, as in the national language, for what amounts to the same object. The *yo-yo* of the 1930s is at present the *return top*, autogiros of those days (actual and toy ones) have become *helicopters*, *bathing costumes* have turned into *swimsuits*, and Sir Oswald Mosley's *National Party*, which at that time antagonised many Cockneys by insisting on marching through the East End, has at least some parallels with today's *National Front*. A change of name does not always prove a completely new thing.

In vocabulary, London still uses a number of very unorthodox terms. Here is a preview of some:

beedle, beetle, binny heavy
  mallet
beever meal out
birch brum besom for sweeping
  leaves, etc.
boss-eyed, craws-eyed cross-eyed
bowk to belch
clatter to chat, to gossip
cack-'anded left-handed
clog, scotch wooden chock to
  prevent cart or car going
  backwards when stopped on
  a hill
crease water-cress
draw, wet, steep brew (tea)
draw(f)t, dry spell, dry time
  drought
duddakin, privy, closet old-
  fashioned outside earth-
  closet. The first of these
  words is typically Southern
  and East Midland, but
  times change and nearly
  everywhere in London now
  they have been supplanted
  by the modern *loo*.
earlywig, airwig earwig
effit newt
ever-slit, 'angnail, snag loose
  piece of skin at bottom of

finger-nail
emmit, pissimire (older) ant
flittermahs bat
frut untidy person and *frutty*
  untidy, e.g. 'She's frutty'
gapin' yawning
grahts, grahnds tea-leaves
jippoes, gypsies
moggy cat
oddny-dods garden snails
'oppin' the wag playing truant
picture-palace cinema
pin-toed pigeon-toed
pollywag tadpole
skew-ways, cater-cornered
  diagonally, e.g. 'Yer've 'ung
  that picture skew-ways'.
shuck, uck pea-pod
slack, sleck coal-dust
snob cobbler
spraw-footed, bat-footed splay-
  footed
straddle-legged astride
sway-gog, titsy-tot, tippeny-tawter,
  see-saw
tine prong of digging fork
totter itinerant scrap-merchant,
  rag-and-bone man. Older
  Cockneys know him well.

It is interesting, however, to see how many words of supposedly Romany origin are well established in Cockney. Here is a list, with the Romany parallels in brackets: *Bloke* (Hindustani *loke* 'man' via the gypsies); *cock* 'friend' (*kak* 'uncle'); *cosh* (*kasht* 'stick'); *cove* (*covo* 'that man'), *dekko* 'a look round' (*dik* 'to look'); *lolly* 'money' (*loli* 'red', i.e. copper, coins); *pal* (*phal* 'brother'); *rum* (*ram*, originally 'man', then 'queer man', then just 'queer').

Actually the first two are of doubtful origin. *Bloke* could be from Dutch *blok* 'a fool' and *cock* from the Anglo-Saxon *cocc*, imitating the bird's crow, that helped to make *Cockney*. But enough common words are in the list to show that Cockney's Romany element is larger than might be imagined. Thus, if you hear 'Ave a *dekko, pal*, at that *rum bloke* carryin' all that *lolly*: 'e might get *coshed*', many of the words are not only Cockney but true gipsy.

Nevertheless well over 90 per cent of Cockney words, including nearly all the tiny but important link words such as *and, at, but, by, of, in* and *to*, are from Anglo-Saxon. Therefore, if you are accused with 'Yer great lumberin' clod-'opper' (awkward ungainly person) or 'Yer as deaf as a man wiv no ears', you might console yourself with the thought that all the words are prime Anglo-Saxon and of great antiquity.

Dialect

Some folk argue that London lost its dialect centuries ago, but a scrutiny of Joseph Wright's 1904 *English Dialect Dictionary* shows that this is untrue. Here are some examples from that great work of words he notes as then current in London. Some, though classified there as dialect, lie in fact on the boundaries between dialect and technical language, but they show indisputably that London had its own vocabulary:

bobbing-charge payment of a penny by a Billingsgate porter for the privilege of carrying bought parcels of fish for the buyer

Boroughman inhabitant of Southwark. A *Wappiner*, a *Mile-Ender* and a *Boroughman* were 'terms used about the Exchange and Fenchurch Street, to express an inferior order of beings'

bouncer professional beggar (not in the modern sense of a *chucker-aht* at a London club)

brancher young bird scarcely able to fly

buff to strip to the skin

bunter rag-gatherer

canary sovereign, from its colour

coaly coal-porter (*cf* for its ending modern London *dusty* dustman and the Scottish *postie* postman)

dowzer a tip (French *douceur* sweetness; gratuity)

dung underpaid worker

fried carpet fried fish and potatoes

greedy-guts glutton

hockey a game similar to golf, the ball being a knotty piece of wood

jowler sparrow

keeler wash-tub

leek inexperienced chimney-sweep

mutcher pilferer

pensioner blind street-musician

pimp small bundle of chopped wood for firelighting

poke-face a mask

sank-work the making of soldiers' clothes

scamper jerry-builder

scrunch to crush, e.g. 'I don't like being scrunched up in the corner.'

shore-man, shore-worker one who searches sewers for rats, etc.

skinnum a trained pigeon

sludder mud, mire

specks damaged fruit – street traders' term.

stand pad to beg in crowded busy streets with a written statement round one's neck, such as 'Wife and five kids to support'.

tat gatherers rag collectors

trailer prowling cab-driver

woolwite yellow wagtail

To such may be added many others in current use, like *scrumpin'* (stealing) apples, a favourite pastime for boys; *cubby-hole* for a snug corner; *leather* and *paste* 'to thrash'; to *lollop* (lurch) *abaht*; *ninny* 'fool'; *oddments* 'remnants', such as those at *jumbo sales*; *shammy-leather* (chamois wash-leather); *swap* (exchange, barter); and *traipse* 'walk in a trailing, untidy way'. A Cockney mum will turn on her *kids* with 'Wodyer come traipsin' in wiv all that mud on yer boots for?' Cockney talk may be based primarily on modified Standard English with a large mixture of slang, but its historical dialect element cannot be ignored.

People

There are surnames special to the London area. If you come across people named Cornell (i.e. Cornhill), Fulham, Hammersmith, Harfield, Hounslow, Kensal, Staines or Turnham, you can be assured that their ancestors came from Middlesex. Essex surnames include Rumfitt (i.e. Romford) and Tilbury; and to Surrey belong amongst others Lambeth, Mitcham, Putney and Tilford. London itself, a very old surname, presents little of a problem although very few natives bear it compared to the numbers of those surnamed from other towns and cities such as Bedford, Chester or York. Contributing to this scarcity of London as a surname may be the fact that the city, which even in Anglo-Saxon times was of great importance, grew too large to have an easy identity.

A change in how a surname is spelt or pronounced may baffle

more than it should. In 1978 Mr John Cuckney was appointed the new chairman of the Port of London Authority – most appropriately, it would seem, as his surname resembles *Cockney*. Other slight changes in spelling, like the surname Plaister from Plaistow, can be puzzling. Non-Cockneys have trouble understanding the local pronunciation of various surnames, such as *Ahd*, *Fahz* and *Mahny* which stand respectively for Howard, Fowles and Mahoney.

It is striking that of the five most numerous surnames of people resident in London (which are in order of frequency Smith, Jones, Brown, Clark and Taylor) no less than three are occupational; and of these Clark and Taylor do not figure even in the top 20 surnames of Cardiff, Dublin or Edinburgh[8]. This implies, as one would expect, a rather greater proportion of skilled workers in London.

Nicknames are popular, except usually with those who bear them. Costermongers were rarely known by their real names but, as Mayhew points out[9], by such appellations as *Dancing Sue*, *Fishy* (a seller of fried fish), *Gaffy* (once a performer), *Whilky*, *Foreigner* (who had served with the Spanish Foreign Legion) and *Curly* – this last is still popular in London, but now, for example for West Indian girl immigrants with frizzy hair. Costermongers' nicknames were usually acquired in one of four ways, namely from:

a) some mode of dress (e.g. *The Toff* from his rich clothes)

b) generally remembered remarks (e.g. *Brassy*, a very saucy person)

c) some peculiarity in trading (e.g. *Pineapple Jack*; *Spuddy*, a seller of potatoes)

d) a striking personal appearance (e.g. *Dirty Sal*, costermongers generally objecting to dirty women).

Taking names from the twentieth century and outside the costermonger circle is easy. *Billy Flappers* was a long-eared Whitechapel boy who probably hopes never to be reminded of his nickname. *Rubberneck* was a man who swayed from side to side apparently in perpetual motion as he played the piano at the silent pictures. *Monkey Brand* was a man whose face unfortunately resembled the monkey on the advertisement for that rubbing stone. One East Ender used to push a wheelbarrow selling *'addicks* and shouting 'All mild!' (i.e. not salty). From his cry he was nicknamed *All Mild*. *Burglar Bi-oo* (Bill) was till recently a sarcastic East End name for the people at the local tax office at *Feevin'* (Thieving) *Lane*.

The *-y* ending of nicknames like *Smiffy* 'Smith' indicates a certain friendliness. *Stitchy*, named thus, was a docks character. How he received his name I do not know, unless it was for putting bystanders into stitches of laughter. Men working with him used to shout, 'Stitchy, what time d'yer make it?' Stitchy would not answer but would move the peak of his cap in various directions, e.g. for '1.30 p.m.' he would move it to where the figure 1 would be on a clock face and then pull it right round to the front position.

Current examples include *Keys* for a market key-cutter adorned with an enormous ring full of keys, *Swede-basher* for anyone from a remote village or looking like a country yokel, *Freddy the Fly* for a notoriously lazy dock worker, and *Mrs Effer* for a Whitechapel woman notorious for her swearing. Nowadays most Cockneys saddled with nicknames have acquired them from some personal characteristic or incident of their schooldays, like *Ginger* 'red-haired', *Bony* who is thin, *Tubby* who is like a tub, or rotund (thus also Tubby Clayton, London founder of the Toc H movement), or *Chopsy* who talked too much. Some of the nicknames are ironic, as *Lofty* for a tiny person and *Tich* for a tall one, and *Sunshine* or *Sunny Jim* for a person with a face like the proverbial wet week. Yes, a lot of importance lies in nicknames.

For people met on the streets many special names have blossomed. The *oky-poky man*, a name surviving in the 1930s, was the ice-cream seller on his tricycle bearing the well-known invitation 'Stop me and buy one'. *Costermonger*, however, was a pre-1914 word. Between the wars they were known by their separate occupational titles. There was *de rabbit man*, *meat man*, *fish man* and *winkle man*. *Of a Sunday arternoon* 'On Sunday afternoon' there also appeared, e.g. around Millwall streets, *de comic man*, who sold five comics for an old penny, and *de muffin man*. Nowadays any such street-seller, whether man or youth, is simply a *barrer-boy*. Similarly in London's East End a *newsboy* can be an adult, though even that term is less confusing than those in the Meadows and other working-class areas of Nottingham, where a *paper-lad* can be of any age and either sex.

The guardian of the law is in traditional Cockney the *co(pp)ah* with a disappearing unexploded *p* – a word which long ago supplanted the older one *bobby* from Sir Robert Peel, chief founder in 1828 of the London police force. He is a *co(pp)ah* because he *cops* or catches, and police informers, a detested breed, are *co(pp)ahs' narks. Fuzz* and *pig*, also in use, are very modern terms. The equivalent of the ancient London *footpad* is the *muggah*, who violently steals from people in the street. East End victims do not usually complain *I was mugged*, but *I got set abaht* or *got done up*.

On a bus, *conductress* is the official and usual title, though sometimes the affectionate term *clippie*, which arose during the last war, is still heard. The official remover of household waste is no dustbinman or, as officialdom would have us believe, a garbage disposal person or environmental officer, but simply a *dusty*. One of my best informants was a retired Hackney *dusty*; and if like me you had had the privilege of listening to them, e.g. at a strike meeting calling themselves by the same term, you would have no shadow of doubt.

Those dark-skinned people who often come round begging have in the metropolis at least three names which have to be carefully distinguished from each other. The *pikies* (named from hop-picking families?) live in settlements, the *diddiguys* are those of mixed marriage, and the gypsies proper are of full Romany descent.

The man with horse and cart, who scours the streets shouting 'Owd ahn (old iron), rags bo(tt)les an' bones!', is *to(tt)ah*. Having met *trotter* amongst other words for this gentleman in other cities and hesitatingly even in London, when I saw *totter* in a *Sunday Express* article I began to wonder whether it could be a misprint, but informants leave me in no doubt. *Tro(tt)ers*, they maintain, are pigs' feet. Also irrelevant is the name *totty*, which in some British cities stands for a prostitute.

Financial personnel included the *sales feller*, nowadays termed a *rep* 'representative'; and the *tallyman* 'debt-collector', who came round houses each week for money. Cockneys also met a *tallyman* in the Kentish hop-fields.

Bookies had their *runners* on street corners, waiting to relay illegal bets, a practice now rendered unnecessary by the opening of betting shops. The grandiose designation *turf accountant* for someone who will take bets, e.g. on election results or holiday weather as well as horse-racing, is a modern invention. This is not to say that *bookies* were, or are, less clever than their colleagues in the more respectable part of the accountancy profession, and this remark applies to one of my helpers. Son of an East End publican and right-hand-man of a *bookie* at New Cross and other *dogs*, he maintains that a quick-witted able assistant is vital to level the books and to keep the *ol' firm* solvent. Such reasoning cannot be faulted. In Army days this very pleasant fellow carried his skill abroad, where for example on leave and almost *cleaned aht* at Brussels racecourse, he turned certain peculiarities of the track and the positioning of runners to his advantage. By this I am not suggesting that Cockneys are by instinct *Joe 'Ooks* 'crooks', just that with few exceptions they are very alert, as their hard life and residence in the throbbing capital have trained them to be.

New words like *commi* for a trainee chef have not established themselves in the East London heartland. Neither has the title domestic servant ever been popular since no-one likes to be most remembered for serving and obeying the slightest whims of superiors. In very large houses there would be the kitchen maid, cook, butler, footman, etc., supervised by *de ahskeeper*. Now she is merely someone who calls, perhaps weekly, to keep one's house clean. Work in the more menial jobs used to be harder than it is today. It would be said of a *grafter* (hard and willing worker), 'She works like a black', which would now be thought racial, though it sets coloured people in a good light.

The *potman* of the 1930s was usually a part-time waiter, trying to earn an extra *bob or two* at week-ends. There was the *carman*, driving a horse and van, and the dreaded bailiff. A Cockney *clerk* was, and still is, pronounced to rhyme with *perk*, as the spelling helps to show, though actual perks in lowly jobs were precious few. Nowadays Cockneys trained as *brickies* 'bricklayers', *chippies* 'carpenters, navvies', or *sparks* 'electricians', provided they have not lost their jobs to become *dahn-an'-ahts*, can earn very sizeable wages.

Next we investigate names of people associated primarily with their habits. Someone who often drinks excessively is said to be a *boozah* – ''E comes 'ome when the pubs shut an' they chuck 'im aht'. An untidy and dirty female who ''angs fings up on de floor' is a *sloshpot* or ironically *Mrs Tidy*, with her house *any owd 'ow*. Ironically again, someone in a bad mood is 'a 'appy owd soul. She'd be a good advert in de funeral parlour – she's gor a contract wiv 'em'. A man over-fond of money is a *miser*, not a *skinflint*, and he 'Chucks fings away like a man wiv no arms'.

Tart used to be an affectionate word for a young woman, but according to Partridge's *Dictionary of Historical Slang*, by 1904 it was being used only of loose women. Although that is not wholly true (I still hear it very occasionally in the old respectable meaning in

Northern towns), it certainly seems to have been so in London. In the early 1940s, 'Look at those tarts over there' caused consternation in a high-class North London hotel. A later Cockney word for such a woman was a *brass*, shortened from *brass knob* and referring to the old iron bedstead with four brass knobs. It is still sometimes said.

In the 30s round some East End streets as the barrel-organ played there would appear to perform a short high-kicking dance men dressed as girls and called *nancy-boys*. This has become a well-known term for men with effeminate tendencies. For homosexuals the current Cockney is a *poof* (tramps' cant from about 1870), or euphemistically ''E's de ovver (other) way'.

Children's dialect words are especially significant because by their frequency we can estimate how strongly the local speech is likely to survive. By such a yardstick Cockney still has a long future. East End *kids* can still play havoc with acceptable English, as when they return from school reporting 'They're learnin' us to read' or 'Remember (remind) me to get that comic'. *Learn* and *remember* in these senses have at least the historical support of Shakespeare and the Bible.

They are a pugnacious breed, which helps to account for all the terms for hitting. One lad will threaten his *mate* in the playground, 'I'll gie yer a punch up de bracket (on the chin)' or 'one on de 'ootah (the *hooter*, nose)'. His *mam* will warn him, 'Yer dad will pay (chastise) yer when 'e comes in'; and dad on arrival will say he is going to *wallop*, *larrap* or *tan the 'ide orf of 'im*, or if lenient simply *give 'im a clump*.

The exasperating *kids muck up* wallpaper by smearing their dirty hands all over it. They seem to be always *moanin'*, *naggin'* or *botherin'*, in contrast e.g. to Manchester ones who keep *mytherin'*. They keep screaming and crying, despite parental orders to 'Stawp yer racket!' or 'Owd yer rah (Hold your row)!' They are far too *saucy* 'cheeky' and give too much *lip* 'impudence'. They are usually up to mischief, *frowin'* or *chuckin'* stones. They enjoy being free, especially about four o'clock when school *is aht*, but regrettably some snatch extra freedom by the time-honoured London custom of *'oppin' de wag* 'playing truant'. However, some do get on very nicely at school and work, for which the height of praise is the typical remark ''E's it' or 'She's it''

Games do keep them for long periods relatively harmless. All sorts of *baw* (ball) games are popular, whilst the toddlers love the see-saw, also called a *titsy-tot* or *tippeny-tawter*. They used to sit in East End gutters playing *gobs an' bonsters*, a marble game where the *bonsters* were thrown up and, if they were successfully caught, a wild grab was made for the larger *gobs*, which had been placed on squares. Another game was that where someone jumps onto the backs of several children as they crouch, hands on the shoulders of the person in front, facing a wall. For this game, a London term is *Spanish leapfrog*, but, as it was a boys' game, it is hardly surprising that Cockney girls who saw it being played in season all around them knew it simply as leapfrog. Children derive such intense pleasure from games that it is a shame to see their opportunities of this kind so sadly curtailed by London's dense and still growing street traffic.

The Cockney family centres politely upon *fahver* and *movver*, but in practice upon *dad* and *mam*. Some aspiring Cockney mothers actually encourage this swing to the more familiar names by insisting 'There's no *f*s (They really mean *v*s) in *mother*', at which their fond children take the easy way out by responding *Mam*! Children also call their parents, but not to their faces, the *ol' man* and the *ol' gel*.

The very old generation is represented by *granfahver* or *granfahder* (both pronunciations still active) along with *granmovver*, or more familiarly *grandad* paired with *granny* or *nan* (short for *nanny*).

Whereas Lancashire and Yorkshire use *our* to describe members of the family, Cockneys prefer *my*, e.g. in the understatement 'My Mary don' 'alf get up my 'ootah (i.e. she greatly annoys me)'. *My boy*, which is popular, e.g. in *Danny boy*, *Johnny boy*, is due apparently to the influence of many Irish in the area. It is applied also to dogs. '*Ere, boy*! a man will try to cajole his enormous dog as it yaps at a stranger's ankles, hoping with the stranger that it will respond like a child.

Apart from *brovver*, which admits him to a much wider fraternity when he is so addressed at union meetings, all people connected to the Cockney by birth – sons, *dau'ers*, aunts or aunties (with of course 'long ah'), cousins, etc. – are his *relations*, *relatives* being the polite and lesser-used word. By observing their faces on, say, a wedding photograph you can often see how well relatives *take arter* each other, or *favour one anovver* (which my helpers say is the 'simplest way' of putting it).

Son- and daughter-in-law are also too polite and vague for normal conversation, where for instance a mother will talk of *my Kaff's* (Catherine's) *Jimmy* or my *Bert's Ada*. Similarly *my husband* and *my wife* are unnaturally polite expressions. If you ask *Missus Smiff* at her door whether you may borrow her lawnmower, she will probably say, "Tain't my job. I'll ask de ol' man'; whilst if you ask her husband for some milk, he will probably say, "Tain't noffink to do wiv me. I'll ask de ol' gel' or 'de ol' Dutch'. This last is many a Cockney's term of endearment for his life's partner – and he means it. Yes, family trees are one thing, accurate only historically: families in the flesh are quite another, as Cockney language shows.

The body

We are all interested in living bodies, especially our own, and the Cockney is no exception; but first two general points have to be made. One is that for the body the vocabularies of Cockney man and wife noticeably differ. He it is who commonly uses *gob*, *conk*, *mawlies* and other slang, doubtless through the influence of his *mates* at work, whereas his *ol' Dutch*, who is much more often at home and more subject to the refining channels of BBC radio, resorts to them very rarely indeed. Secondly, a reason for much slang collecting round the head and face, as in 'I'll bust yer conk' or 'I'll smash yer gob', is that when tempers run high and the urge to hit is barely controllable, the surface of politer speech cracks. With a possible recipient of the blows right in front of him, the Cockney often instinctively accompanies such threats by appropriate gestures.

Let us start logically with the head, the power-house of lively Cockney activity, and work downwards. The head may be his *napper*, *bonce* or *nut*. Somebody with reddish-yellow hair, which according to taste makes her attractive or slightly ridiculous, is a *ginger-nut*.

Associated with the head are powers of thinking. Anyone with limited brain matter, always doing foolish things, is *simp-u* 'simple', *dotty*, *daft* or *nuts*. He is a fool or a *prat*. Anyone completely out of his mind draws the diagnosis that he is *potty*, *crackers*, *awf 'is rocker* like a broken armchair, or *awf 'is nut* possibly like an unsecured bolt. Naturally if he is merely *merry* or *boozy* 'slightly drunk', or has *'ad anuff* or is *one over de eight* 'is very drunk', his fuddled brains have a very different reason.

Some words connected with thinking have no exact translations in Cockney. *Conceited*, it has been reported, is in use amongst schoolchildren at Highgate, but lower down the hill at Islington the equivalent is the circumlocution ''E finks well of 'imself'. This is evidently a class distinction. *Capricious* is similarly a word used only by the better educated, ordinary Cockneys substituting descriptions like 'She keeps changin 'er mind' or 'Yer never know when yer've got 'er'. Likewise 'She's inquisitive' of suburbia becomes in, say, Shoreditch 'She's a righ(t) nosy Par(k)er'. For 'untruthful', a polite Cockney way to speak of a person's statement is 'It's all a bit of moody', i.e. imaginative but untrue.

Those who seem confused are in a *'tis-was*, i.e. not knowing whether it is now or then. Others are *dead scared* 'very frightened'. When it comes to intelligence no finely adjusted measures of I.Q. are needed, for as the Cockney says folk either know what they are doing and so are *wiv it*, the *it* being commonsense; or else they do not and are labelled *wivaht it*.

A variety of expressions encircles the hair. If long and un-combed, it quickly gets *scruffy* 'tangled'. A Cockney goes to his barber's to *'ave a 'aircut*, not to have a *pow* (from Dutch *poll*) as is still said up North. But the Dutch word still exists in London sayings like ''E's a good poll (has a good head) of 'air'. Other sayings prove the importance of hair, for it excites much pointed comment when it grows in an unusual fashion: ''E's growin' past 'is 'air' (said by children of a man blessed with hair only at the side and bald on top); 'showin' yer 'airs awf' (showing off, boasting); ''E's carrying' a nanny' (i.e. *nanny-goat*, beard); 'Get a comb froo yer wool!' (Comb your hair!); ''E's got luvverly 'air, all dahn 'is back' (of a bald-headed man).

Eyes, nose and ears, if at all unusual, also take their share of unkind remarks. Some unfortunates are *boss-eyed* 'cross-eyed'; whilst others with outstanding nasal organs have Jewish noses, pug noses, Roman noses, or simply *'oo(t)ers* or *big conks*. Strangely, despite Heathrow Airport, the *Concorde nose* for a type of prominent nose, though used in other British cities such as Carlisle, has not yet embedded itself in London language. With ears, linguistic usage varies. Only a minority of the over-60s employ the Scandinavian word *lugs* for ears. I have heard it claimed by a veteran Cockney that *lugs* is 'posh', but what he really meant was that it was unnatural to him. The word is more firmly established around London docks for the gills of a haddock, and stands (like the nautical *lug-sail*) for anything that has to be pulled. Cockneys also use *flappers*, but not the East Midland word *tabs*. For the part inside, the choice lies between *'ear-'ole*, *burr-'ole* and *lug-'ole*. Any will do. E.g.: "'E's gor a cauliflahr 'ear-'ole'; 'Yer burr-'ole's red'; 'Smash 'im rahnd the lug-'ole'.

Gob is one word for mouth, but *mahf* is commoner. To quote a line from a famous Cockney song, 'Lummy, wor a mahf (Good Lord, what a mouth) yer've got!' Ladies who over-use their mouths for talking and spreading tales are 'cha(tt)erboxes, proper ol' gossipers, awlus na(tt)erin''. In the Cockney's mouth, something may be wrong with a front *toof* or with his *back teef* 'molars'. Another minor complaint from around the face and neck makes him become his own doctor by *bustin' the 'eads* (cores) of boils. Another type of complaint, but not always a minor one, comes from Cockney mothers insisting that their *kids* wash away the *tide-marks* (lines of dirt) round their necks.

More Cockneys than ever seem to be *cack-'anded*. This is because modern education, unlike many of the old elementary schools, does not force children to use their right hand. The father of one of my informants used to say: 'We're all cack-'anded 'ere – Dolly's laid the table', because she used to put knives and forks the wrong way round. She still eats like that although, like many a reader who is partly *cack-'anded*, she draws straight lines and uses scissors with the other hand. The expression for left-handed, though also found elsewhere, is definitely typical of the London region, and of places within it as far apart as, say, Harlow New Town and Old Coulsden in Surrey.

Hands occasion other unorthodox words, for they besides feet can be the sites of *corns* 'callosities'. They have *fumbs* and a Cockney-born Army rifle instructor, angry at his recruit's slowness in releasing the safety-catch, will be well understood when he shouts, 'Flick it orf wiv yer fumb!' (The rest of his remarks might also be somewhat unorthodox, but not specifically Cockney). In the East End the piece of loose skin at the bottom of a fingernail, for which Standard English seems to have no special word, is an *everslit*; whilst a person who cannot do things properly with his hands is *awk(w)ard* 'clumsy' or in extreme cases 'as awkard as a ruptured duck'.

Dealing now with middle regions of the body and its associated states, we notice first people who are *umpty-back* 'hunch-backed'.

The *belly* is the whole internal digestive area including the stomach. Consequently 'I've gor a right pain in mi belly!' may herald only a mild bout of indigestion. If that results from eating too greedily, the sufferer is called, shortly and expressively, a *gut*. For the reverse, if he is very hungry he is *starvin'* and if very thirsty he is *dry*. If he watches *Orient* or *The 'Ammers* (West Ham) on a frosty day without his *smovver* (overcoat), he will be *froze* 'very cold'.

Through the help of improved medical science few people are now seen with gross deformities of legs and feet, but some are still met who are knock-kneed, *bandy*(bow)-*legged*, or *pin-toed* or *'en-toed* 'pigeon-toed', or who have *quarter-past-free feet* (are splay-footed). Whatever the shape of their poor legs and feet, if they have scorned cabs and carried heavy suitcases great distances towards Liverpool Street Station, they will plead, 'I must have a rest, I'm beat' (or *tired aht, fagged aht, done for, done up* or *knocked up*), or explode with something stronger like *right buggered* 'absolutely exhausted'. Here for lack of space this section closes, though as may be readily imagined, especially from the last despairing examples, our published results of variant Cockney terms for the body and its states are far from exhaustive.

The Jews

London has been rather more tolerant of Jews than have other British cities. For example in 1837 London University allowed them to take degrees, whereas Oxford and Cambridge refused until the 1860s. Beyond the academic world London as a whole has appreciated them more, partly because they have been so much needed in its financial and textile communities.

Whitechapel language has been greatly influenced by its large Jewish population, though it is now rare to find a foreign-born Jew in the locality. The synagogue on Commercial Road used to be the only one putting on plays in Yiddish. Most Whitchapel Jews, being of East European descent, know some Yiddish, a mixture of German and Hebrew which is classed in the Dewey decimal library system as a Germanic language. Not surprisingly the intermingling of Jew and Britisher has resulted in East Enders being conversant with an unusually large proportion of Yiddish, German and Hebrew words.

For example *shicksa* (from Hebrew *sheques* 'blemish') is Yiddish for a non-Jewish woman, especially a young one; and this is what one of my Wapping-born-and-bred aids was called when she attended a Jewish synagogue wedding. She understood quite well the word with its meaning because it was part of the district's general culture. *Shobbas* (Yiddish *Shabbes*) was the Jewish Sabbath, from Friday to Saturday sunsets, and so unusual to Cockneys of English origin for whom it was a time, not of *tittivatin'* oneself, parading the streets and going to the synagogue, but if they were lucky of relaxing after a hard five-and-a-half-day week by perhaps going to watch Millwall at The Den or by going shopping.

J.B. Smith reports[10] like me that, even if only peripherally, gentiles took part in some of the Jewish festivals. One of his informants states on tape, 'And in the Jewish religion there used to be a holiday called Purim. Now in the religion – of course I'm Church of England – they used to have confetti, flour, and as children we used to go round and throw at people – you know, the confetti, not the flour. And when it was their Passover we used to eat the matzos'. This unleavened bread (Hebrew plural *matzath*, Yiddish *mott-sez*), very thin and about four inches square, I heard as *mottsaz*. Doubtless alternative pronunciations are possible.

Quite a number of food names are current outside the Jewish community for which principally they were baked – *bagel, holler* and *pletsls*, for example, along with *mottsaz*, which are enjoyed not only at the Feast of the Passover but daily in various *caffs*.

Guyver is another Jewish-sounding term. If an acquaintance tells you 'Yer've gorra lot of guyver', you are what most East Enders would call a *show-awf*, a boaster. Appended are some of the typical London Jewish words known to Christian people settled in the environment. Note what a large proportion are disparaging:

Cockney pronunciation in approximate spelling	Meaning	Derivation
bagel	hard, doughnut-shaped roll	Yiddish *bagel*
benkl	little stool	*Cf.* German *Bank* 'bench'
bubbler	affectionate name for a child	Yiddish *bubeleh*

faird	fool	*Cf.* German *Pferd* 'horse' especially in the sense 'cart-horse'
gelt	money	German *Geld*
gonov	thief	Hebrew *ganov*
holler, collar	braided loaf of white bread	Hebrew *challah*
klutz	oaf	German *Klutz*
mashiggener	slightly mad, *tapped*	Hebrew *meshuggener* 'crazy man'
pletsl	thin, flat, crisp roll	Yiddish *pletsl*
schmerel	silly	*Cf.* Yiddish *shliemel* 'fool', origin doubtful but said to come from a leader Shlumiel (Numbers, chap. 2) who was always losing
schmuck	oaf	German *Schmuck* 'ornament', probably used ironically
schmutters	rubbish	Polish *szmata* 'rag'
schnozzle	nose	German *Schnauze* 'snout'
shekels	coins	Hebrew plural *shkolim*. The word appears in Shakespeare (*Measure for Measure*, II, 2, 'Not with fond shekels of tested gold')

An investigation of the speech sounds of such Jews is more confusing, as a study of older writers would show. According to Professor Brook[11], Charles Dickens appeared to believe in about five typical mispronunciations, namely loss of *r* after a consonant, *t* becoming *d* between vowels, the *f* in *of* being absorbed into the initial *b-* of a following word, and the lisping of *s* and *z*. Instances of all five features occur in *Little Dorrit* when 'an elderly member of the Jewish persuasion' takes Arthur Clennam to the Marshalsea prison when he is arrested for debt, and speaks only five words, 'a tyfling madder ob bithnithz (a trifling matter of business)'.

However, other writers have highlighted additional features. Mayhew[12], referring to the language of London Jews around Petticoat Lane, mentions their invitations to buy the *sheepest pargains* 'cheapest bargains', with *sh-* for *ch-* and *p-* for *b-*. Other differences in their speech can also be discovered. Those that always intrigue me are their apparently wayward uses of grammar, like *in search for* to mean 'in search of', and their over-abundance, even sometimes in the pulpit, of business expressions like *in the red* 'in debt'.

Yet to most hearers the distinguishing marks of their speech are, quite justifiably, the individual and sometimes alarmingly isolated words. For example, a *benkle* for a stool seems to demand a scrutiny of the object to make sure exactly what it is; whilst, if you are called just *Schmuck!*, it sounds worse than *Lout!* or some other English equivalent. That is why special attention has just been drawn to the strong Jewish and Yiddish language element in the traditionally poorest parts of London's East End.

Other nationalities

A whole book or even a small library of them could be written by experts on the language of overseas immigrants to London; but the important principle to grasp is that – so far, at any rate – far from significantly influencing London speech, their own languages are being modified and then swallowed by English.

Bearing in mind the widely different origins of the immigrants – the West Indies, Malaysia disgorging, e.g. its 'boat-people', the Arab countries, Nigeria, India, Pakistan, etc. – and their manifold languages and dialects, it would be most odd if linguistically they could band together to press out any common form of English. That said, however, there appear minute by minute, to anyone cocking an alert ear, all sorts of oddities and differences in their attempts to grapple with the English of London and its East End.

As a woman motorist, forgetting her indicator, violently swerved round a Stepney street-corner narrowly missing us both, a middle-aged man from the Middle East said to me in anger, 'She goes rahnd, she don' show de lightin''. Obviously he had mastered the pronunciation of his new surroundings, but had still to learn the technical vocabulary.

Normally what happens is that words change first and then pronunciations start to alter. For example after a fairly long time, vessels moving along the Thames will cease apparently to be a type of animal, *sheep* to a French settler. Then adjustments will start to appear in grammar, although these also are slow and linguistically painful.

Most difficult to change, and beyond the powers of most immigrants settled in London for decades, are stress and intonation. They are so deeply engrained in the speech patterns of their native languages that they are almost impossible to remove when speaking English. Queen Mary College and other East End establishments of high learning may do their level best, but they cannot work the impossible. Through the more level stressing of their languages, the *t*s of an Indian or Pakistani student saying for example 'I want a toasted teacake' shoot out like bullets, and 'Take two tickets to Tottenham Court Road' is said with equally rapid fire. Cockneys should never smile at these errors in a superior way, for the educated Cockney (an alleged contradiction but there are now plenty of them) cannot use his 'O'–level French or German to pass himself off in Paris or Hamburg as a Continental.

Many giggles arise on London Transport about the way our overseas brethren handle the names of places they visit. They travel to *Blomley* and *Blentford, Soutend, Bummansley* (Bermondsey), *Luddergate* and *Ackaton* (Ludgate and Acton), *Pushey* and *Prixton* (Bushey and Brixton) and by Epping Forest at *Taydon Boys* (Theydon Bois). Best of all were three Pakistani lads travelling on their own and gabbling away 'nineteen to the dozen' in their own laguage until the conductor came for their fares and one said in impeccable Cockney, 'I want free Befnal Greens fer me an' mi mates'; and, when the conductor asked where they had got on, they proved their abode, without doubt, by saying together *Lime' ahs* in pure Cockney fashion.

Children born in London of an overseas father and an English mother are more inclined to the mother's way of speaking. This follows the pattern of fully English descended children, who are usually more speech-influenced by their mother simply because in their early childhood they spend so much more time with her.

To examine the speech of every overseas language community in London would be a mammoth and almost impossible task. One would have to consider what used to be said in *Chinatahn*, as the Chinese sat smoking on the steps of their houses. One would be forced to note and analyse quite un-English remarks like the Gaelic *doom the dorris* 'shut the door', often said by an informant's *nan* 'grandmother' who was born in Cork but moved at an early age to Stepney. Spanish influence would have to be reviewed, and Italian, and any Russian, and so forth, which would be wildly beyond the aims of this work. The reader can only be encouraged to consult if he wishes and as they appear specialist surveys like J. C. Wells's thoughtful and detailed study of *Jamaican Pronunciation in London* and to remember the principle with which this section began, that the key to the situation is London English breaking down the speech stock of overseas immigrants and not vice versa.

To illustrate the kind of thing that is constantly happening, let us assemble a few findings about West Indian English in the capital. Far more than particular words, it seems to be certain vagaries of syntax and differences of pronunciation that intrigue or startle a listener.

High on the list of peculiarities is the use of *isn't it?* or the Cockneyised *ain't it?* as an all-purpose enclitic or tag-question symbolising 'wasn't it?', 'didn't they?', 'shouldn't I?', 'couldn't we?', etc. For example, 'It was guaranteed fer a year, isn't it?', 'They went awf, ain't it?', 'I should go there, isn't it?', 'Couldn't we go nah, isn't it?'

Omission of the pronoun *it* seems very typical; for example, *Is* (It is) *very good*. But there are all sorts of unexpected manipulations of phrase and sentence, such as 'Gawn to Cannin' Tahn to live?' and the answer 'For truth' (truly, certainly). They would take pages to enumerate in detail.

Intonation is another striking difference. It has never been thoroughly analysed because the process is so difficult; but it would not be at all hard for you, as I do from time to time, to make an elementary musical score to remind yourself or anyone else of how someone's voice went up and down, as in the diagram on p. 45. This should be enough to show you whether the pattern is English or not (Scottish and Welsh people are useful material here, with their habits of high-rising intonation at sentence ends, so that many an ordinary statement like 'I live here' sounds like a question).

West Indians tend to retain many un-English sounds. Their creole (sub-language) has differences such as short *o* in words like *shot* 'short'; initial *t-* for the unusual sound in most world languages of *th-*, as *tink* 'think' corresponding to Cockney *fink;* a 'thin' clear *l* finally in words like *ball* as against Cockney's 'dark' *l* which often

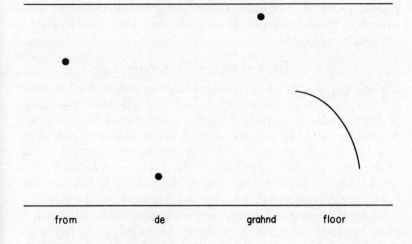

from   de   grahnd   floor

changes to a vocoid *u* making it into *baw-u*. Creole's *er*-vowel in
words like *early, certain, first, work, burn* has lips more rounded than
Cockney's.

In words like *day* and *know*, during the *ay* and *ow* the tongue of
the islander speaking creole drops slightly to make these sounds
into falling diphthongs, whereas the Cockney's tongue in the same
words rises to make closing diphthongs. To put it more plainly,
Creole *day-a* 'day', *knaw-a* 'know', equal Cockney words sounding
rather like *die, now*.

Wells classifies his informants into four groups thus:
1 Jamaican creole
   (uneducated Jamaican)
2 Jamaican English
3 Received Pronunciation (Standard English)
4 Cockney
His most important conclusion, which bears too on other languages as they mix in London English, is as follows. Jamaican
creole and Cockney are at opposite ends of the scale. In other
words, a Jamaican English speaker is much nearer to Standard
English than a creole speaker is to Cockney. It does not therefore
follow that an uneducated Jamaican and a barely literate Cockney
have much in common except the social stigma of being unable to
use the accepted speech of their countries.

From the foregoing it will be quite clear that to lump all London

English speakers irrespective of race, religion and colour into two sharply defined categories of true Cockney and non-Cockney is well-nigh impossible.

Greetings and farewells

These are quite varied. Typical for meeting people are *Ello, mate! Ah yer bin?* (How have you been?); *Ah are yer?* (How are you?); and *Wotcher!* (Hello!). Favourite ones for parting are *So long, then;* and *Be seein' yer* (with *I shall* understood) or much more often just *See yer!* The last can also mean 'I might see you again some time'. If it draws the mournful reply 'Yes, I will', it is no criticism of the first speaker but probably just an acknowledgment of the fact that they both have to return to the dreary round of work on Monday. *Bye!* (Goodbye!) is a softer farewell, generally reserved for use between *ladies*, as Cockney females prefer to be called, or between the women and their *kids* – sorry, ladies and their children.

Common terms of endearment are *mi ol' china*, for example to one's wife or male friend; and amongst men *mate* 'workmate; companion', *guv* (short for *governor*), *boss*, *chief*, *general* and *squire*. The last five of these appellations are rather flattering, sometimes chosen for safety as the quickest ways of establishing good relations with a stranger. Though moderately friendly, they always have a slightly ironic air about them, as if the Cockney knows that the stranger he is addressing is not so elevated in society.

An older way of addressing a stranger is with *mush*, as in ''Ere, mush, can yer give us a 'and (help me)? 'Another salutation which still has its adherents is *tosh*, but this is rougher. It was once much affected by *spivs*, the *wide boys* (cunning men) who made quick profits in the wartime black market. Shortly afterwards it became a great favourite in the Army and a general form of address in the East End. It remains mildly provoking, like digging you in the ribs or some ways of clapping you on the back. It could be connected with Scots *tosh* or Cornish *toshy* 'well-dressed', which is what the *spivs* thought they were.

Yet another greeting is *cock*, as in *Wotcher, cock!*. The first part of this greeting apparently includes a shortening of the country gentleman's greeting 'What cheer!', but the second part is socially quite different. A cab-driver will tell a fare, 'That'll be two quid, cock'. This *cock* is not from *Cock Robin* of the nursery rhyme but from another well-known bird, the chirpy *cock-sparrer* which darts about

London. There is an older form *cocky*, as in 'Don't you believe it, cocky; it ain't nothing of the sort'[13], but this is much rarer.

From time to time some of these greetings cause annoyance. Quite a number of people, especially *toffs*, dislike suddenly being addressed as *Jack*, e.g. by a garage mechanic, whatever their Christian name. At others some workmates show mild surprise. A maintenance *wallah* I passed was asking, 'Ah are yer, mi ol' flahr?', to which his *mate*, admittedly a bit long in the tooth, replied, 'Yer should call me ol' weed'. A similar exchange occurred with a Euston railway porter I heard objecting to being addressed as *Hello, son*! He grumbled, 'Call me grandad', which certainly seemed to fit his age and that of many of his British Rail colleagues. More dangerous even than *son* is *boy*: a *ree-u* (real) Cockney will resent *boy* from a younger man, as I think most of us would.

A worker will talk about his *mates* (the usual term), *the lads*, or more elegantly his *friends*, e.g. 'I met one of my mates' (he is not a bigamist!); 'I'm goin' aht wiv de lads' (even though they are adults) or 'wiv my friends'. In addressing them, the first two expressions are quite in order ('Come orf it, mate.'; i.e. 'Stop it!'; 'What's up', i.e. 'What is the matter, lads?'). In such a context, however, *friends* would sound absurdly polite – he would be courting ridicule to ask 'Friends, what pub shall we proceed to next?'

Some common greetings are quite alien to Cockney, whilst others, as we are witnessing, are very typical of it. Addressing a lady, a Cockney bus- or cab-driver unlike his Northern counterpart may be reluctant to say *love*. It is sometimes used, as a friendly term to both friends and strangers, but never by man to man as can, it seems, genuinely occur in the North and North Midlands. A Cockney, however, will certainly not be so outlandish as to employ in these circumstances the South-Western *m'dear* or the Tyneside *hinny* or the Scottish *hen*. He may call her *deary*; *duck(s)*; or, especially if she is young or small, *pet*. These are frequent, e.g. 'It's free o'clock, dearie'; 'I'll see yer accraws de road, duck' to an elderly lady, though she is not necessarily waddling like a duck); 'What's the matter, pet?'

Cockney greetings may rise to the heights of apparent romance. 'This way, darlin', says a middle-aged office worker, opening a door with his foot to let an attractive young lady enter. Generally speaking, however, that term is trendier and middle-class. Another rather fanciful one, but used occasionally, is *chuck* (Only when you have had some of the alternatives pointed out do you begin to realise how many there are).

Certain of these endearments are not without their literary associations, several having been publicised by Shakespeare who of course wrote for London audiences at the Globe Theatre. *Chuck*, originally a call to chickens as it still is on English farms, occurs in Macbeth's warning to his wife, 'Be innocent of the knowledge, dearest chuck'[14]. Note too how many of these endearments, including *cock*, are animal names. Another apparently is *brahma*, or *brahnger* 'girl-friend'[15] The reason is that, just as people are generally kind to animals, so they try to be to the people they address in the same fashion.

A quite different opening is *Nahthen*! Despite its apparently crazy formation (how can it possibly mean 'now' and 'then' simultaneously?) it is a useful greeting, either of endearment or more often of warning as when it is shouted to Cockney *kids* spotted crawling over the bonnet of your new car. But *Oi, 'oppit, you*! is more effective, particularly if the shouter is agile and follows with a rush in their direction. *Ey up!*, which does fine service in the mining areas of South Lancashire and Derbyshire, is hardly in the Cockney phrase-book.

Another contradictory-looking matter, originally pointed out by Matthews[16], is the Cockney's habit of using terms of lechery as endearments – 'He's not a bad old sod' or 'the poor little bugger'. The original meanings of the key words are toned down by the generally favourable nature of the comments.

Apart from the *Nahthen*! type illustrated above, which is usually a special case for a special purpose, Cockney terms of address in their cheerful variety generally achieve their aim, to strike up fast a warm, friendly relationship.

Comparisons and other sayings

London has its special comparisons. Old ones are: 'They agree like the clocks of London' (in other words they do not); 'as old as Charing Crawss (Cross)' or 'as old as Paul's (St Paul's) steeple'. *Wardour Street English* refers to a street off Oxford Street once noted for its spurious antiques, and meant false snobbish attempts at Standard English. Nowadays for this a Cockney may say 'She's talkin' right cut-glass', or ''E's talkin' peas over sticks', as if he is growing too high like an over-ambitious pea-plant.

Modern comparisons include: 'as clumsy as a coot', 'as daft as a wagginload o'monkeys' or 'as daft as they make 'em'; 'as fast as a church' (e.g. of a rusty nut); 'as 'ard as nails', 'as lahsy as a lahse' (what indeed can be lousier, i.e. more detestable than a louse?); 'as smooth as a baby's bum (bottom)', 'It's like sleepin' on a gravestone' (very hard). In north Stepney, where within living memory there were *cahsheds* 'cow-sheds', a favourite comparison, vying with 'fat as a pig' and 'fat as a porpoise', is 'fat as a cah'.

The word *London* appears in fewer sayings than might be expected. Famous remarks about it refer mostly to its mass of people and endless variety. Disraeli called it 'London – a nation, not a city' and said 'London is a roost for every bird'. Nicholas Grimald in *The Lover to his Dear* showed his dislike of 'people-pestered London'; but others have been appreciative, for example Samuel Johnson who stated 'When a man is tired of London, he is tired of life', and Joseph Chamberlain, who in a 1904 Guildhall speech proudly claimed 'London is the clearing-house of the world'.

Where sayings about London betray an especially notable gap is in so rarely daring to brand the city as peculiar relative to other parts of Britain. For instance, a *Manchester screwdriver* is a hammer, unless you happen to live in Manchester, where it is a *Brummagem screwdriver* on the principle that only people so foolish as to be born in Manchester or Birmingham would work to the motto 'If you can't fit it, hit it'. But I have not personally heard of a *Lunnon screwdriver*. Similarly there are *Derbyshire neck* 'goitre', *Devon splits* for a type of slightly sweetened bun, *to come Yorkshire* 'to cheat' *to do a Shevvild* 'to run away', *to Welsh* 'to refuse to pay' (a term which angers many Welshmen), *Manchester sunshine* 'rain' and *Newcastle hospitality* for the sort which kills with kindness; but little equivalent for London. It seems almost as if the rest of the country is afraid to name London in its comical and proverbial sayings.

A good proportion of the sayings about London which have gained prominence have not been made by Londeners. *London dressing*, which generally meant soot, was a term from Hertfordshire. *To do a London flit*, meaning to move house stealthily at night without paying the rent, was a Derbyshire term. Londoners themselves have never used it: like most Britishers they say for this odd but sometimes necessary operation (a striking example of which I noticed about a year ago not far from my home) *to do a moonlight flit*. *To rear like London puther* meant to assume airs, to be conceited, but it originated in the West Riding; whilst *to put* (or *show* or *turn*) *the best side to London*, meaning to make the best display one could, was clearly used by provincials in some awe of the capital's splendour. Northerners, especially the ladies, say disdainfully, 'London wouldn't be London if the Queen didn't live there'.

To various London districts special sayings have been attached. From the nineteenth century we find *to have been sent to Blackwall* for having a black eye, *Whitechapel play* for cheating in billiards and hence any game, and *Billingsgate pheasant* used jokingly for a red herring or bloater. As Tyburn was in the parish of Paddington, there were *Paddington spectacles* for the cap drawn over a criminal's eyes at his hanging, and *dancing the Paddington frisk* for being hanged. Most of these district sayings are euphemistic, sounding better than what they really represent, like the two Paddington ones and the more modern *I'm goin' to Kew Gardens* for 'I shall have to join the queue'.

Turning to more general sayings, *On yer bike!* 'Clear off!' seems a little out-dated in the modern car age but is still popular, whilst the not-too-original "E must have met 'er (of an ugly woman) when it was foggy' is still in vogue. However, today's Cockneys in free conversation keep providing plenty of arresting rejoinders and snatches of philosophy. For example from a docker's daughter came 'The shame in 'im 'd turn a shit-cart over' – modified after a glance at me to *muck-cart*; 'Yer fink I'm senseless 'cos I got (have got) no sense'; 'If there's green in my eye, it's a reflection from yours'. A saying of some Cockney workers who strongly believe in the value of good food for a growing family, is 'Give it to 'im: aht o' the belly they grow'.

Sometimes speakers do not realise how preposterous their innocent remarks sound. A football fan patient at a North London mental hospital was inquiring 'Ah's Arsenal gawn on?' 'They lawst'. 'Don't tell the rest of 'em 'ere: they'll go mad if they know'.

Although London depends less on the weather than do country villages, it too has weather sayings, like 'The moon's wet – it'll rain tomorrer'. Or, when the rain is *teemin' dahn* (pouring heavily), Cockneys cut the gods down to human size by complaining. 'They're doin' their washin' up there, they ain't (haven't) sent it to the bagwash (laundry) this week'.

Above all, many of the sayings reflect Cockney wit: 'I'll go to get mi false teef sharpened' meaning 'I should be angry but I can't'; 'She's made up like fried bread' (of a woman enveloped in gaudy clothes, or resplendent with copious lipstick and *eye-shadder*); 'She never opened 'er purse, 'case a moff'd get in it'. Linguistically, London sayings are important to show words not mummified in glossaries but in lively action. But beyond that they are vivid, and fascinating in their own right.

Coarse words

Any consideration of the crudely vulgar side of Cockney must take into account the swear and sexual words that punctuate the speech of a good many individuals. They have little variety. *Bloody* is still the most frequent; *bleedin'*, *blinkin'* and *flamin'* are others, e.g. 'It's a bloody shame'; 'Git orf yer bleedin' 'igh 'orse' (Don't try to be superior); 'along the blinkin' alleyways'; 'Where've yer put that flamin' spanner?'. All have practically lost whatever meaning they once had (*bloody*, for example, is supposed to be shortening of the old Christian oath *By our lady*!), and as a rule they just convey an air of mild irritation.

Exactly the same applies to sexual words. *Bastard*!, a spectator will shout at a referee awarding a penalty against *The 'Ammers* 'West Ham United', *The Gunners* 'Arsenal' or *Spurs* 'Tottenham Hotspur'. This does not however mean that the referee's birth was illegitimate. 'That bugger's goin' ave to come aht', snarls an East End electrician grappling with a screw; but the screw's offence is not a moral one, only that it is too tight.

Some people put coarse-sounding terms into every two or three words they say, but in such profusion they can convey, at most, only general annoyance. They come from people with rather limited vocabularies, and if you listen to a cross-section of Cockneys you will soon recognise the words. Many people are shocked at meeting them, especially when they are being used by Cockney children who, if their words were taken literally, would seem obsessed with the crudest bodily functions.

Swearing is naturally not a new phenomenon. If the meekest Cockney male drops a concrete slab on his toe or the kindest-hearted mum finds that the Sunday dinner is burnt, something harsh will be said, aloud or mentally. Pent-up feelings need an outlet. Cockney women indulge in far less swearing than men, one factor doubtless being a fear that it will handicap their children's careers. Typical is this housewife's statement: 'I 'ate swearin' – it's common (low-class). A woman swearin' is worst: a man yer can stand'. Yet some of the women interviewed, very friendly though they themselves were, gave vent to what seemed the unfriendliest coarse language, from *My Gawds*! and *run like buggery* to far beyond, although in their defence it can be argued that their extreme words had lost their historic meanings.

Disturbing, though, is the apparent increase in swearing. Schoolboys now swear and some schoolgirls. In the 1930s a spectator at some London football ground would curse a 'clogging' player on the visiting side or some wretchedly inefficient member of his home team; but now young soccer fans indulge in chanted swearing. It is said to be growing more sophisticated, which in technique it may well be, but it seems senseless nevertheless.

In London as elsewhere the building industry has always had a reputation for swearing; but others, such as car-manufacturing, can run it close. In theory, one would expect the Cockney to swear much less than his fellows in the provinces because the East End has no coal-mines, one traditional haunt of the crudest words, and sends a good part of its work-force into Central London offices, especially those devised on the open plan where words travel so easily to the fair sex and anyone not meant to hear them, that swearing is taboo. On the other hand, life in London lived at a quicker pace than by, say, farmers or rural postmen, can be undeniably more frustrating.

Billingsgate in particular has been singled out as a home of swearing, though it seems exaggerated to blame so much on such a small market area. In fact today, as heavy traffic lumbers by its main entrance, it is hard for anyone there to hear himself swear. But Gayton in 1654 was noting 'Most bitter Billingsgate rhetorick' and, according to Partridge's *Dictionary of Historical Slang*, to *talk Billingsgate* meant to indulge in foul language.

Strong language has been making many unexpected appearances. According to a *Sunday Express* report,[17] an international defender who need not here be named was sent off the field at Stamford Bridge, Chelsea's ground, for using what was called 'industrial language' to a linesman. More astonishing was a report in the same paper[18] from an ex-head and member of the Bullock governmental committee into reading and the use of English that a

London-area teacher was alleged by a parent to be in the habit of dismissing his mixed class at the end of the day with the earthy colloquialism *Piss off*. It rightly states that, where a teacher is prone to easy acceptance of debased norms of speech and writing, his own personal standards are likely to be dangerously eroded. These cases are exceptional but show a dangerous trend.

Swearing appears to be becoming more direct. Formerly most people swore rarely and many not at all, and much of the swearing was quite mild. You might have heard, 'Nah, yer young galley (galley-slave, i.e. rascal), Cor Blimey! What yer doin'?' or 'What the nation (damnation)!', plus a sprinkling of *darns, dashes* and *drats* (euphemistic alterations of *damn*) and possibly a *Gock (God)!* that now would hardly be classed as true swearing. Things have changed. Recently I noticed a man who was walking with two young sons on one side of a road suddenly whip himself into a fury to shout at civil servants opposite on strike, *Ger orf yer arses'*. He must have meant it metaphorically, for they were standing! And a short distance farther on the speech arising from a hole in the road was unprintable.

Oaths differ from area to area just as normal dialect does. For example, the shortening *By*! (for *By God*!) is typically North-Eastern and *By gum*! typical Lancashire, whereas London's nearest equivalent is *By Jove*! Comedians and others make efforts to revive moribund oaths with only limited success. In Lancashire the comical *Ee, ecky thump!* is to all intents and purposes extinct, but in London some of the old oaths, though gradually being supplanted by newer ones, have survived rather better. Such are *Strike a light!* and the emaciated oaths *Struth (God's truth)!* and *Cor Blimey (God blind me)!*, generally abbreviated to *Blimey!* Besides being expected – one might say almost compulsory – in revivals of old-time music-hall, they are still around in ordinary conversation.

But, like the hordes of chanting fans on the soccer-ground terraces, individuals are becoming more original in their selections of oaths or quasi-oaths. For instance, one London police inspector never (at least at home) used obvious swear words. His favourites, in order of preference, were *Cor, love a duck!* (again we have *Cor* for 'God'); *Cor, stone the crows!*; and *Good green gardens*! I have heard the last from no-one else, though a contributory factor may well be that he had moved to Kew.

Any Cockney is at liberty, one would imagine, to swear or not to

swear; but, if he must, then it should be done effectively. To insert a
swear word into the midst of two others reveals a certain limitation
of vocabulary; and to make every other word a swear word, as
some do, destroys whatever meaning they every had. Without
wishing to sermonise on the one hand or favour swearing on the
other, it needs to be said that if Cockney swearing – or for that
matter any other kind – is to be of use, its words should hold
recognisable meaning.

Malapropisms, etc.

Into the reckoning must come slips of speech, of the kind Mrs
Malaprop kept uttering in Sheridan's play *The Rivals* and from
which they called malapropisms. Genuine ones appear in
churchwardens' accounts, wills, inventories, etc., e.g. 'uppon his
owne Apperill (apparel?, peril?)' in St Mary-at-Hill minutes for
1642. For centuries they have aroused much amusement. From
Elizabethan and Jacobean times, dramatists have loved to poke
fun at the Londoner's love of impressive words. For example in
Shakespeare's *Henry IV Part II* the Hostess tells Pistol 'aggravate
(ameliorate) your choler', and in 1613 in Beaumont and Fletcher's
Knight of the Burning Pestle Spaniards are mistakenly called *Spaniels*.
     To the unfortunate Cockneys who now utter them malapro-
pisms are simply great embarrassments and the sooner forgotten
the better. Cockneys seem ill-at-ease with long Latinised words
and fear confusing them. This is why distressing speech-traps lurk
especially round doctors' waiting-rooms, where you hear from
time to time of complaints like *very coarse veins*, *Arthuritis*, *not enough
haemogoblin*, 'I'm sufferin' from nerves and high potential (hyper-
tension), or very commonly *bronichal asthma*; and suggestions like
'Give 'im an enemy (enema)'. A very unmechanical driver, again
from the London area, told his friends (who told me) that his
garage had located trouble with the *deferential and exhilerator*; whilst
a central London informant reports that when he was a small boy a
Cockney woman told his mother to rub his chest with *Venus turps*,
and only years afterwards did he discover that she meant 'Venice
turpentine'.
     Noting malapropisms is an interesting task. The *jumbo (jumble)
sale* is sometimes heard, and it sounded even odder in an elderly
woman's remark 'I'm givin' that sweater to the jumbo'. Some are
merely mistakes of pronunciation, like *pronounciation* itself (a

common error, even amongst students), *architect* (with a *ch* sound) and *tarpoleons*, rhyming with *Napoleons*, but for tarpaulins.

Worse are the usual type where a whole word goes astray, e.g., 'This library's quite restive (restful)'; 'Yer a septic'; 'The great metrollops (metropolis)'; 'Give 'im a momentum when 'e retires'; 'collector of internal residue'; 'Spuds is mi stable diet'; 'Gerrawf: it's the turnimus'. Their actual percentages in Cockney speech are small, but the disturbance they cause to it and the barely controlled titters they can excite are out of all proportion.

Still rarer speech gaffes are the spoonerisms, where heads of words change places, such as *Go-men of the Yard* 'Yeomen of the Guard'; *mice of sleet* 'slice of meat'; I'll 'ave some of that stink puff (pink stuff)'; *Kate an' Sidney (pud)* 'steak and kidney pudding' and *in a ruddy blush*, 'bloody rush, great hurry'. These errors are extraordinary because, although it is common enough by thinking ahead to say one sound before it should rightly occur, it is remarkable to transpose a pair. Spoonerisms were first recorded in South-East England, as the word comes from the speech failures of the Rev. W.A. Spooner, who was Warden of New College, Oxford, until 1924. They are unusual mistakes, but made by everybody sometime.

Far more serious, because of the weird logic they show, are what might be called London Irishisms. You will soon recognise the type. Examples: 'Is anybody sat on that chair next to yer? (indicating one that is clearly empty); 'It's a five-minute walk to Liverpool Street if yer runs'; 'Is that the jelly we 'ad for tea?'; 'Whadyer 'ave that toof took aht for?' (pointing to the gap); 'See that road turnin' left? Well, it's not that way, it's the ovver'. Two elderly inhabitants reported to me that, when they remonstrated with a young Cockney mother for leaving her baby in a pram in cold weather outside her admittedly tiny flat, she replied, 'I've gotta pur 'er 'ere for I've got nowhere to pur 'er'.

These Irishisms seem far worse than glaring faults of English or arithmetic, for how can anyone live efficiently if he does not think straight? But in fairness it should be said that the words slip out before they can be recalled and there is no real need to question Cockney intelligence, which is at least as sharp as that of anywhere else in the British Isles.

The 'foreign' element

Cockney vocabulary has also what might be termed a foreign element, by means of which anything unpleasant is blamed on another country. Thus we find *Chinese overtime*, paid as overtime but starting at an unusual part of the day before normal working hours. Regrettably Cockney builders and decorators, like many others of their trades, include in their ranks a significant number of those who are fond of *workin' foreign*, i.e. working, sometimes in their normal employer's time, on private jobs for which they are paid in cash unknown to the Inland Revenue. Yes, London has its fair share of *forriners*, though many are born and bred in the heart of the city.

The backwardness or oddity of those from overseas is suggested in other ways. From Lords to the most unpretentious cricket pitch in the capital a snick through the slips is a *French drive* and one to fine leg a *Chinese cut*. Yet it is not so remarkable, for we English ourselves do not escape being branded as foreigners. For example, to quote again from cricket, if you are in Australia our *French drive* becomes a *Chinese drive*; and in the United States putting spin on the ball (a crafty move) is *putting on English*. London boroughs have their *Dutch auctions* where the bidding drops and *American auctions* where part of the proceeds go to charity, neither therefore being counted a true auction. The stomach disorder likely to attack visitors to hot countries has many names, including *Delhi belly*, *Rangoon runs* and *Tokyo trots*, showing incidentally the fondness for rhyme and alliteration[19]. But the Cockney and English *French letter* equals the French *capôte anglais*; in schoolgirl colloquial French *Les anglais sont debarqués* 'The English have landed' stands for 'My period has started'; and *la maladie anglaise* is V.D. whereas to other Continental nations the 'English disease' is that of strikes. We are not the only nation to take terms for embarrassing ideas from other countries.

Of course, there is a sense in which vast stretches of Cockney language sound foreign – that is, to overseas doctors practising at the London hospitals and in the East End. They learn with difficulty to understand the language, much of it euphemistic and a good deal of it slang, in which their patients try to describe their complaints. 'To die' is *be a goner, conk aht, 'ave 'ad it, peg aht, push up daisies, turn it in, turn yer toes up* (This has been used for over 50 years), or *kick the bucket* (coming actually from the slaughter of pigs, Old

French *buquet* being the beam to which the pigs' legs were tied and no bucket being involved). 'Slightly drunk' may be *fresh, squiffy, tiddly, tight*, etc., and 'very drunk' *soaked, sozzled, stoned* or *parlatic* 'paralytic'. Phrases describing pregnancy include many that are rare in polite society, such as *bein' up the pole, 'avin' a bun in the oven, bein' in the puddin' club, bein' in pig* and *bein' preggers*. To feel unwell is to be *aht of sorts, groggy, awf colour, run dahn, wonky*, etc. For doctors from overseas, Cockney does amount to a foreign language, and it is surprising that they understand as much as they do.

Space-fillers

About 20 years ago every Cockney conversation seemed well larded with 'so I turned rahnd an' said . . .', which tended to leave the listener giddy trying to follow mentally the gyrations of the protagonists. But this is not the chief weapon in the armoury of the speaker who wants instinctively to delay making a pronouncement until he is sure what to say. Very frequent, and for many of us unfortunately unavoidable, are the *ers* and *ums*. In print they hardly appear, but when dealing with real living Cockney – and nearly all of that is spoken – they must in fairness be considered. They correspond to the Scottish sentence-plug *aym*, and for some speakers can be quite a hindrance. To try to kill this habit, some *movvers* tell their *kids* 'They killed the bull fer 'ummin'', although this warning is also given to those who *um* when not paying attention.

Great rivals in usefulness to the *ers* and *ums* are *yer see* and *yer know*. In fact, some of those prone to *er* and *um* defend themselves – how honestly is hard to determine – by claiming that their space-fillers occur only because they know the right word and are just searching for it, whilst Cockneys who can think of little to say except *yer see* and *yer know* lack *eddication*.

Be that as it may, it does not complete the list of available sentence-crutches. There is *Righ'?*, used abrasively as so often by Army instructors. Another filler is *an' that*, e.g. 'Yer've gotta be social (sociable) an' that'. An interrupter for listeners but a delayer for Cockney speakers is *like*, which is often a great favourite with those seemingly short of ideas: 'It's like this, like. That man-like come up to me an' said-like. . . .' *Well. . .* , according to a *tec* I know, is the commonest word with which criminals begin their confessions, although it is not usually written down like that at

Wapping police station or Bow Street Magistrates' Court. *Sort of* and *kind of* are further well-known examples, with which we'll sort of lead this analysis of space-fillers in a typical Cockney conversation towards a close. It is far from a digression – it is forced on us by their sheer number.

Sign language

A trap is to imagine that all Cockney language, apart from a few painfully written letters and hastily scrawled shopping lists, is verbal. Yet there is another important side, the use of signs and gestures. When a Cockney after talking business tightly clasps your hand, that means 'It's a deal' or, if you are cynically minded, 'That's to make sure you don't get out of it'. A shrug means something; as do a wink, a nod, a shake of the head and without doubt a blow of the fist. There is holding the nose with one hand and pulling an imaginary chain with the other to indicate a *no-good* or *wash-aht* (utter failure). If a Cockney, man or woman, gestures by turning a finger in the ear, this indicates that another person present is *on de ear-'ole*, i.e. anxious to borrow something and listening for a suitable opportunity to be lent it and then probably keep it.

Much of the sign language has to take place in noisy occupations where it is more effective than attempted verbal exchanges, e.g. in ship-repairing, heavy engineering and textile mills. It is essential as much to the *tic-tac* man signalling how the betting is progressing at New Cross *dawgs* as it is to the *copper* on point duty near London's *Tahr*.

Another important aspect of it is that cultures vary tremendously in tabooing certain ideas in ordinary language but allowing them in kinesics (sign language). Cockney is no different. For instance, what is often delicately termed 'making a proposition' is difficult, nay impossible, to verbalise to, say, one's young lady on a seat in Finsbury Park. With appropriate signs it is still very probably the wrong thing to attempt but slightly less embarrassing. It needs more thought, as does the whole matter of sign language.

Market jargon

London is well-known for its street markets, the most famous being that in Middlesex Street better known by its old names *Petticoat*

Lane or just *The Lane* and close by Liverpool Street Station. Traders take pride in how long they have been in business there, a stallholder claiming, for example 'I stood the Lane 20 year'. Cockney market jargon has always been interesting, but it changes as old methods die and new ones take their place.

Pitchers 'stall-holders' working with their *'anders-aht* 'handers-out' who watch for thieves and distribute goods, are becoming rarer. The *oilclawf wallahs* 'oilcloth-sellers' used to do a roaring trade, conducting a *Dutch auction* where the bidding goes down, and accompanying each drop in price by a bang of their hammer on the goods being displayed. Now, however, better floor-coverings are sold in furniture shops and the *oilclawf wallahs* are almost forgotten. Similarly, with the coming of the National Health Service, quack doctors or *flahry crocuses*, who used to sell various pills and potions which they claimed would cure almost every illness, have disappeared.

Though many a modern trader still uses a special *patter* 'line of talk' to entice customers, and though *pitch* still means his place of trade, the jargon has changed greatly. A *ganawf* or *ganovvin* was a thief, a term hardly heard nowadays. *Gazumpin'*, notorious in the 1972 housing boom and to a lesser extent in 1979 for beating a rival purchaser by offering above the previously agreed price, used to mean on the markets a less socially disruptive action, 'to diddle in a nice sort of way'.

Gear means the saleable goods and having a *flash* is having a big stock on display. Being *in the jungle* means that a stallholder finds his goods hard to sell because he is hidden from public view, having to stand perhaps between a second-hand stall and a trader selling curtains. The warning ''E's comin' rahnd for the toby' is a signal to have the stall rent ready for the collector; and *doin' a bomb* occurs when trade is really brisk and a seller cannot possibly go wrong. A walk round any Cockney market to listen to its words can be most enlightening.

The following chart, which is from an Inland Revenue circular used in the London area, contains an interesting specialisation of the word *price*. Still more important, it shows that, whether you simply want a good bargain or whether you are officially checking traders' activities, it is much safer to understand their technical market terms.

APPENDIX TO BN 19   MARKETMEN'S JARGON

The following are words commonly in use among market traders and Inspectors may find it helpful to know them. As with most jargon, it is unwise to take the initiative in its use but it can assist the Inspector's credibility if he understands it when it is used by the trader.

BAT	Price. When buying goods, marketmen seek to avoid 'full-bat'.
BUNCE	Profit. A 'buncy line' is one carrying a high margin.
BURSTER	A market that attracts vast crowds of customers.
DONE IN	Sold out. Is used of individual terms, e.g. 'had a buncy line but it's now done in'.
AN EDGE	Usually refers to the price paid by the tracer to his supplier and means a small price reduction.
FLASH	The stall display; visual attraction.
FLYER	Very popular line that sells well.
FLY-PITCHERS	Experienced traders who gather crowds by their spiel (called 'pitching'), frequently working from the back of a pantechnicon.
GAFF	Market or fair.
KITE	A cheque.
A PRICE	Means a *low* price. Traders ask for a 'price' from their suppliers.
PUNTERS	Customers, or potential customers.
STICKER	Line not selling well.
SWAG	Flash lines; usually unbranded goods. Cheap but attractive lines.
TOBY	Stall or pitch rental. (Or short for 'Tobyman'.)
TOBYMAN	Market Superintendent, or his assistant.

3
General Vocabulary: Mainly About Things

Clothing

For clothes worn beneath the rest, elderly Cockney women use the modern word *undies*, but otherwise they cling to older expressions. If someone's underskirt is showing, they will warn her 'Yer slip's lookin' aht'. They talk not of bikinis but still of *bathin'-suits* as was customary in the 1930s. Next to the skin they wear a *chemise*, or in the case of a few very elderly women what they call a *shimmy* (anglicised pronunciation of the last) or a *shift* (another name for it).

For a Cockney working-man the corresponding item of apparel is usually a vest, since he reserves the older *singlet* as a name for sportswear. His cap, called in Yorkshire a *flat 'at* and in Belfast a *duncher*, is his *cady*. On London docks as with London stationmasters, bowler hats were for high officials. They were a mark well up the social ladder to *give 'em a stattus*.

Now we come to the Cockney's *trahses* (alternative *rahnd the 'ahses* – 'Yer can't go aht wivaht them'). They have to be secured by what he usually calls braces, but sometimes flippantly *Epsom races* or *kings an' aces*. Above them may be his *weskat, jacket* (preferred to the shop-term *coat*), and his *smovver* (i.e. smother) or *topcoat* 'overcoat'. Yet another word for the last article, though rare now, is *'owster*, i.e. 'holdster'. If children were slow getting ready for a winter walk, fathers would urge them, 'Get yer 'owster on an' ger aht quick'.

The pockets of a Cockney are especially interesting to a word-collector. The old word is *flap* – 'I'll pur it in mi flap'. Another is *bin* – 'Gor any money in yer bin?' A third way is to use rhyming slang, as when he tells his wife, ''Ere, mi ol' china, come an' sew up this ole in mi sky rocket'.

When it appears in Cockney clothing terms, slang – both the

61

ordinary and the rhyming kind – can be rather disconcerting. Someone has a *smashin' pair o' wheels*, which turn out to be boots; another has trouble with his *dir'y faces*, which are only shoe-laces.

Here it might be as well to stop; for if we moved on to dressmaking terms, like *brizz* for a type of pattern in lace or *rooleau* for a special kind of binding on a dress, the explanations might prove too intricate for a mere male to unravel. So let us leave well alone.

Equipment

Equipment includes the *beedle* or *binny* 'large mallet' with its *and-u* 'handle'; *wee-uz* 'wheels'; and the *'ammer*, occasionally called in a weirdly repetitive way a *'and-'ammer*.

To most Cockneys a ladder is a ladder and that is the end of the problem. But those who have been in the building trade think of its parts separately, e.g. rungs, and *stringers*, the wooden side-pieces. Similarly to them a door is not always a door but a combination of jambs, stiles, muntins, etc.; and a staircase is made of its parts – treads, risers, *kites*, *winders*, and so forth.

A saw is peculiar only in pronunciation, *saw-a*. The wooden frame on which you would saw a log of wood is a *saw-r-in' 'orse*. With older people the radio is still the *wireless*; but an *umberella* usually receives nearly its proper name and very rarely the old word *gamp* despite Mrs Gamp in Dickens. For an object whose name is unknown or forgotten, the normal procedure is to say 'Pass us (me) the so-an'-so' or, if one is irritated, to insert a swear adjective, making it for example, the *bleedin' so-an'-so*.

One of the most remarkable names for an article of personal equipment of decoration is *groin* for a ring on the finger. This, which I met in Whitechapel and again in Woolwich, is apparently not in the dictionaries but might possibly have come from Anglo-Saxon *grīn*, which was pronounced rather like modern *green* and meant a noose or halter. Other items are *bins*. They could be dustbins or, as we see in the clothing section, pockets; but here they are short for *binoculars*, i.e. spectacles. All is made clear by the context.

Vehicles

In London you do not take a taxi, you *catch a cab*. Lorry is pronounced with a short *o* through the influence of spelling. *Mo'ers*, like cars elsewhere, *miss* when they are not firing on all cylinders;

but when they have a poor gearbox, unlike cars in other parts of England which *crawnch, grawnch* or even *scuffuffle*, they *crank*. 'For Christ's sake', an irate dad will tell his learner-driver son, 'Stop cranking that gear!' And, as in any segment of Cockney language, you must never be surprised at a little rhyming slang creeping in. 'Yer too late, cock', a bystander tells a man rushing along the pavement after his friend, "E's caught one of us'. What does that mean – a crime perhaps? No of course, the bus!

Food and drink

Years ago when travel round England was so much harder, it was often impossible for cooks to find out more about preparing food than they could learn from people around them. Before the days of mass media, local cooking conditions were tightly confined to small areas.

London contained many ethnic groups that founded their own communities, keeping their traditions and yet becoming Londoners. So in many parts of London the food was as varied as the people. French and Italians came to London hotels to learn to 'dress salads'. Herbs like comfrey had been used in London centuries before the arrival of Indian tea. Oriental immigrants liked and still insist on their curry, Germans their sauerkraut, and so forth.

Early this century London had nurtured the establishment of chains of food shops such as Maypole Dairies and Lipton's which were household words (*Lipton's fat pig* was in fact the stock schoolboy reply among friends to any unanswerable question, for example: 'Who done that?' 'Lipton's fat pig'). Stimulated by the increasing employment of women, there appeared Lyons teashops with their famous *nippy* waitresses. Now we have East End Wimpey bars, etc. staffed by many hard-working gentlemen of overseas extraction.

A restaurant in Charing Cross Road has advertised 'Four-course typical Cockney "nosh"'. Its food is doubtless delightfully appetising but not singularly Cockney. However, its use of the slang *nosh* is well attested in the East End, where a hungry worker will say to his mate, 'Let's go for a nosh-up' and where, for example, eating-places sprang up like *Norman's Nosh Shop*, just by one of the bridges guarding the Isle of Dogs. Another word which a stranger might mistake is *toak* as in 'What's the toak like?' This does not seem to be the schoolboy slang *tuck* for food as in *tuck-shop*, but means 'dry bread'.

Principally we are considering old Cockney meals. Working-class communities like the Cockneys have established their own distinctive pattern of cooking. They favour large but unpretentious meals, avoiding any extravagant delicacies which could so easily wreck a tight budget.

Beever is a very old word for a meal out, but in the home the names and order of *mee-uz* 'meals' run as follows. Breakfast is succeeded by dinner at mid-day and tea, with if needed supper *late-on*, say about 10 p.m. The Northern term *high-tea* for a tea including a cooked dish is foreign to the Cockney naming system, as is the device of taking *lunch* around noon and *dinner* in the evening, although reference to *lunch* for the mid-day meal is increasing. As for a mid-morning snack, that is normally *break* or (more modern) the 'posh' word *elevenses*, although not consumed at exactly 11 o'clock.

Jellied ee-uz (eels) are a traditional Cockney dish and sold, for example, in shops along Commercial Road. Jellied eels and mash, and pie and mash, were alternatives; but eels are now very expensive and considered a luxury. A speciality of the pie shop was mashed potatoes (called *spuds* or *murphies*) and *liquor*, which was parsley sauce. *Relish* stood for any tasty luxury, usually in food. A wife, trying to entice the appetite of her sick *ol' man* (husband), would say 'I must give 'im a relish'.

There is one important caveat. If as a non-Cockney you are thinking of trying Cockney food, you should do so because you believe you may well like it and that it will do you good. Don't try to copy clients of the Ritz who, as Jack Dash points out in his splendid autobiography, would drive down to East End *caffs* in their Rollses and Daimlers to 'have a jolly hot saveloy, old boy, what!'

Sunday meals were special. However poorly a family ate during the week, they had a treat on Sunday. In the 1930s they might have custard by itself as a sweet – perhaps that was the only day in the week when they bought a whole pint of milk, limiting themselves on other days to a *gill* (half-pint) costing a penny. For Sunday tea the East End custom has been to devour winkles, but now if they do have shellfish they are more likely to be cockles.

There are special foods with London names, like *Chelsea buns*,

To'nam cake, a type of iced sponge-cake, and *Crystal Palace* pudding, which is made from a recipe of 1851; but the Cockney's favourite delicacies are different. Formerly for threepence you could go to the baker's with all your *spuds* and meat covered with a *tea-clawf* and return with it cooked, just having to add other vegetables. The Cockney of today likes *bangers* (sausages) and especially *saveloys*, as mentioned in *Oliver Twist*, the small reddish smoked sausages which used to be sold outside many shops in the evening. *Pease puddin'*, made of split peas, is enjoyed, as are *faggots*, balls of meat-cake made with pork, onions, sweet herbs and flour. Unlike Northerners, the Cockney does not greatly care for tripe.

At the tea-table you may meet one or two surprises – perhaps *wallies* 'large dill-cucumbers' (The *Dictionary of Historical Slang* knows them as 'olives'), or the rhyming slang *Rosie Lea* (from the clairvoyant) or just its shortening *Rosie* for 'tea'. London tea is *made*, *brewed*, *drawed*, *wet* or *steeped* – anything but *mashed* as so often in the North, although the chemical operation is of course the same. 'Wonna cuppa?' you may be quickly asked, with 'tea' understood; or 'Wonna (Do you want a) cup o' tansy?', this last word coming from the name of a herb.

You will be invited to have a *bit*, not *piece*, of bread and butter; but a *slice* of bread and jam. *Roo(k)y* is an old word for 'bread' and a *topper* from its shape is a cottage-loaf. Bread or pastry which has not risen is referred to wearily as *sunk*, though no water is visible. Slices of bread with something in between make a *samwich*, although *sarnie* as in *Sarnie Bar* is creeping into snack-bar titles. Still on the topic of bread, a striking difference between North and South is that, whereas Northerners talk of a *sliced loaf*, in London it is a *cut loaf*.

Rancid bacon has *gawn awf* – you are not told where. The very elderly sometimes talk of *hucks* or *shucks* for peapods, to the puzzlement of their grandchildren. To Londoners the notion of 'ham' is also a trifle confusing. What the North calls simply *'am* is in places like Purley *boiled ham* because there *ham* by itself means cured ham or gammon. However, most dock-area Cockneys could not afford ham, which to them had the same meaning as in the North, and so the need to define it in a corner shop did not occur.

Food prices of the days long before Common Market tariffs now look on paper ludicrously cheap. It used to be possible to get *four faggots fer fruppence* (3d) and *five pahnd o' tayters fer tuppence* (2d).

Some food was actually free. For instance, Johnson's was a baker's shop in Cable Street, Stepney, where in the period 1935–40 one could buy half a loaf (Compare the saying 'Half a loaf is better than no bread'). In those days a loaf of bread was weighed out. In this shop there was added to the bread on the scale a small extra free piece which was reckoned to be a *taster*.

After this linguistic preparation, you are now ready to sit down to a glorious Cockney menu just as soon as you hear the welcome cry, 'Grub up!' (The meal is ready). Enjoy it fully before you have to pay the *Jack and Jill* 'bill':

NOSH

RELISH
jellied *ee-uz* (eels), winkles
or salad with *crease* (cress)

MAIN COURSE
faggot stoo (stew), with *saveloys* and *spuds*

AFTERS
dish of custard
appuz (apples), *goosegogs* (gooseberries)
an' *cracker-nuts* (hazel nuts)

TO SUP
cuppa Rosie wiv a dollop o' sugar,
worth draining to the *grahts* (dregs)
or a pint o' pig's ear (beer)

The house

The narrow path between *ahses* is the *alley* or *passage*. Modern houses, according to my informants, are those built within the last 20 years. This understandably is at considerable odds with what London estate agents appear to believe, that *modern* means built any time after the last war; but estate agents have the tricky task of selling them.

It was surprising to find *terrace 'ahses* a rare term. An elderly Stepney lady explained 'We only 'ad streets of 'ahses. Terrace-ahs was a posh word wiv us in the East End. But it would do for them 'ahses in a li(tt)le quiet part like Paradise Row in Befnal Green'. As for lodgings, a young man would be said to be living in *digs* (abbreviated from Australian *diggings* via theatrical slang, from actors trying metaphorically to dig into their cheap lodgings to make themselves comfortable). Yet a family was always spoken of as being in *rooms*.

Approaching the East End dwelling, you notice door and *winders*, and, if it is *teemin' cats an' dawgs* 'pouring down', perhaps an overflow from the *gutterin'* (gutter fixed to the eaves) and *gutter-pipes* (downspouts). In olden days doorsteps were kept spotlessly clean by intensive rubbing with abrasive stones, and then needed more and more rubbing so that great depressions were worn in them. No stigma was attached to being poor, which was usually inevitable; but no housewife wanted to be thought, from her doorstep or other evidence, a *frut* 'slattern', with a house that was *frutty* 'untidy'.

Of mains services to the house, there will certainly be two and probably all three – gas, *wa'er* and *the 'lectric*. The phone, which for most households has become almost a necessity, has brought in its wake one or two East End language problems. One type is where a dim-witted Cockney on a faint line asks someone trying to spell out a word, 'B for what?' A second commoner and less foolish type can be occasioned by national barriers. A Canadian friend, in Devonshire and on a tour of England, had promised an East End shopkeeper that he would *give him a call*. About 7 p.m. on the appointed Saturday he rang him, only to be told furiously 'Why didn't yer come? I've waited in all day and 'ad to get somebody to mind the shop'. Yet by a slight turn of phrase the Canadian could have been easily understood. If he had said, 'I'll call on you at 3 o'clock', the East Ender would expect a visit and might have asked for a more convenient time; or if he had said 'I'll call you at three', the shopkeeper would expect a phone call. Such extreme examples are luckily few; but, when a Cockney is involved, communication within the English language can be hazardous.

Sections of the Cockney dwelling have special names, sometimes at variance with those of Standard English. The space inside the front door is the *'all*, a name purloined from medieval rooms (*cf* the halls of Oxbridge colleges). Leading from it may be a *passage* (informants insist that *lobby* is a 'posh' word for it, though that would be quite acceptable in most working-class homes up North). The old word for the room with comfortable armchairs where you would entertain an important guest is the *parlour* (from French *parler* 'to speak'), but it is now called the *sittin'-room, front room* or (most modern term) *lounge*. Flats may also have *front rooms*, not necessarily at the front of their block. The downstairs room where the housewife spends most of her time is the *kitchen* or *livin'-room*. *Kitchen* in the East End does not always retain its historical meaning of the room where the cooking is done. What many of us would call the kitchen in the dwelling of one of my *owd ladies* has both sink and oven, but she calls it her *scullery* ''cos it's cowd an' you don't sit there to eat'.

With central heating coal-fires are relics of the past, but the old fire-making apparatus is well remembered – the bellows, tongs, coal-rake, ash-pit, draw-tins for encouraging a roaring flame, and a little trivet for putting the kettle on. Other domestic items should here be mentioned. They may include pictures, hanging *a bit on the slant* 'askew' if the lady of the house has been forgetful with her dusting; *fridges* and freezers; a *poof* (not here a homosexual but that small padded legless piece of furniture); and of course the family god, the *ol' telly*.

Food is kept in the *larder*, not *pantry*, which is thought a 'nicer' word no doubt because it comes from the butler's pantry of country mansions.

Not so nice to mention is the *toilet* or older *lav(atory)*, which over the years has had to keep changing its name. *'Ahs of Commons* was another old word for it ''cos you went there to lobby your MP.' This expression was a favourite with Cockneys whose political leanings were 'left of the left'. The current term is *loo*, but no doubt this will soon be ignored in the search for a still pleasanter name. Some experts, by the way, have always understood *loo* to refer to the cry of former Edinburgh housewives of *Gardy loo!* before emptying the chamber-pots from upper-floor windows. In that case it would come from French *Gardez l'eau!* 'Beware the water!', although there is little connection between unhygienic Edinburgh customs and the East End's improved plumbing facilities -- and why Edinburgh housewives should talk French is a mystery.

Water of a different kind, and plenty of it, was needed on Monday wash-day, which was hard work. In the scullery, scrubbing-boards and *mangles* (wringing-machines) would be in strenuous action. All the house would be pervaded by the smell of escaping steam. But other devices like the *dolly-legs* for beating clothes were rare: the only helpful tools for most women were two strong arms. And afterwards for drying the garments, instead of modern luxuries like spin-driers, laundrettes and outside revolving airers, there was just the *clo's-'orse.*

Some people poke fun at what they call the typical modern Cockney culture of a splendid house interior and an outside toilet, but this criticism is exaggerated. The outside appearance of most East End homes, compared to those of Victorian times, is a vast improvement and sometimes quite attractive. The present-day Cockney housewife works in luxury compared with the times of her grandma. Her *'ahs,* far from being just a drab machine for living in, with its *knick-knacks* from holidays abroad, its eye-level grills, pedal-bins and other labour-saving devices, is blossoming into a veritable palace.

Work language

The Cockney works with his *mates.* They do not actually repair or mend things – holes in the road, *tellies* or anything else. Neither do they *fettle* them as the Northerner does. They *ger 'em fixed* or *pur 'em right.* Covent Garden porters refer to a *head turn* for a small load and the *rave* for the wooden slot on the edge of the *barrer* to retain the fruit. *Scalpin'* is a well-known operation at the hairdresser's which fortunately does not mean taking off all a customer's upper skin. The deposit on a plane iron can be called a *burr.* Billingsgate porters, to empty a truck the quickest way, will talk of *frowin' it over* and, if they have to get boxes from the rear of a lorry, will shout for example, *Free orf de back, Charlie!* These are samples of London's work language.

There have, of course, been many unusual work terms. When London *lumpers* 'casual dock workers' earned about 13/6d a day less *Lloyd George* (their insurance contribution named after the Prime Minister who instigated those benefits), there was the *bompin' office,* a hut such as that which for a long time was in Glamis Road off Cable Street. Here dockers who had tramped in vain from one dock to another in hope of finding work would *bomp on* 'sign on' and so be able to claim what little dole was due to them.

Since, however, there are countless trades and occupations, each with its special terms, we had better give a broader view by moving to general work matters. A pleasant aspect in offices and factories, usually before Christmas, is *'avin' a ding-dong* (party). Another pleasant feeling, which waiters and hotel porters know, is when it can be said, "E's bunged yer', *tipped* being merely the polite word. A custom pleasant and laughable to the older hands but embarrassing to the newcomer is to send a raw apprentice for an impossible object, such as a left-handed screwdriver, a rubber hammer, a tin of striped paint or "alf a 'underdweight o' bread puddin' on a saucer'.

Working normally arouses little comment, but working unusually, either too much or too little, excites a host of remarks. Of a hard worker it is said "E's a good grafter' or "E can collar' or "E's in the collar', like a cart-horse straining inside the collar of its harness. Strenuous work is involved in handling cargo in a ship's hold. Thus stevedores will say "E's dahn in the slave (the hold)'. Informants have seen such work recorded on what was headed the *slave sheet*, the list of companies requiring dockers, although the *guv'nors* officially entitled it the *work sheet*. For an exacting boss there is no set description: he may be a *grabber*, a *right slavedriver* or a *bleedin' guv'nors' man*. The last expression can also stand for a goody-goody person in charge, a *right licker*, who would if necessary grovel to lick his employer's boots. He thinks only of his own promotion, not of you, even if *you was floggin' yer guts aht*.

Working idly is *'avin' it away* or *layin' abaht* rather than *skiving*, which is more of a TV word. Of a lazy person, a fellow-worker might say "E's a right layabaht, 'im!'. Other unflattering descriptions here are a *scrahnger*, someone who has *got no graft*, or a *John Thomas* (to whom this refers I have at present no idea). An idler can also be called a *fly man*, though in this case the implication is that he knows too much and uses his knowledge to dodge duties.

These, naturally, do not exhaust the aberrations from standard working. There is *moonlightin'* for doing an extra paid job after normal working hours unknown to the taxman. With galloping inflation and the advent of the 'black economy' this is prevalent all through the months, whether the streets are bathed in evening sunshine, moonlit, or shrouded in darkness. Systems of extra unofficial work gather different names according to their industry. In textiles it is *cabbage*, in the building industry *the lump*, on fairgrounds *the weed* and in bakery work *skimmin'*.

Goods may be *nicked* or *grabbed*, or more directly it may be said about the thieves, 'They've stole 'em'. If something is repaired unsatisfactorily, it is *bodged up*, *duff* (An Army term), or very simply but bluntly a *lot o' shit* or a *lot o' crap*. Considering all the trials of a working day, elegance of language cannot fairly be expected.

Laws of work have an impact. *Sodd's Law-a*, well-known to Cockney car mechanics, e.g. when no nut will go on, is that *noffink fits*. By *Parkinson's Law-a* every time another *guv'nor* is added to headquarters staff, at least two extra people and two extra rooms are needed because the new *guv'nor* must have a *seccatary*. *Murphy's Law-a* states that, if you miss a bus by a minute, the next will be either half an hour late or perhaps not run at all, as London Transport time-tables used to warn their passengers although they graciously added that officials would do their best to see that buses did come. *McPherson's Law-a* is very similar to Murphy's. By it, if a Cockney falls on a *slippy* pavement and breaks his left wrist, he will be *cack-'anded*; or if in a fit of bad temper he damages his ankle kicking his soccer team's dressing-room door, he will be its ace goalscorer. A fifth law, Driver's and known to every London motorist, is that, if accidents happen, they may be due to other road-users, jay-walkers, passengers talking, fog, the road bending, etc., but can never be his own fault.

Work language sometimes tries to simplify words, but at other times to make them as difficult as possible. To illustrate this, telephonists are familiarly *hello-girls*; whilst in electrical engineering *tweeters* and *whoofers* stand respectively for high- and low-frequency loudspeakers and are formed in imitation of the sounds coming from those pieces of equipment. On the other hand are seemingly unnecessary changes of a technical name. A certain type of wing pliers was in the Post Office called *no. 81s*. This term disappeared officially in 1939 and they are now called by the G.P.O. *pliers no. 2*. However, there is language resistance and Cockney postal employees still call them *81s*.

Industry is not averse to metaphorical language. The Cockney's use of *on tender'ooks*, usually about anxiety in his family, comes apparently from the Huguenot silk-weavers of around *Spi'alfields* where Tenter Square was to be found. Tenter-hooks were, it seems, for stretching the fabric. To take another example, a docker's gang will urge their representative as he goes to negotiate with management, 'give it plenty of dunnage', and if all goes smoothly he will be able to report back to them 'I've laid the dunnage'. *Dunnage* is literally the foundation of matting, brushwood or more often planks used in packing cargo.

Lastly in general work matters let us consider finishing work. At the end of the working day comes *knockin'-orf time* which probably arose from knocking levers away from textile and other machines to bring them to a halt. The more modern method in engineering works and the like is for an *orfice-geezer* (clerk) to watch employees coming out and *clock 'em orf*, although they actually do this themselves by putting their *clock-cards* through his apparatus.

If a job is too hard, whatever the time, it has to be *packed in.* Deliberately staying away from work is *playin' it up* if the idea is chiefly to prey on the National Health Service by getting doctors' notes to confirm minor ailments, or *givin' it the elber* 'elbow' (*giving it the big E* is American). For being dismissed, a Cockney is unlikely to 'get a golden handshake' or 'be relieved of responsibilies'. Less gently he gets the *boot*, *his cards* (literally since his national insurance cards have to be returned), the *poke*, the *push*, or most often the *sack* (from feeling all tied up and finished). Job centres and the government may keep referring mildly to *redundancy*, but this is quite foreign to the East End where people find themselves suddenly and harshly *aht o' work*. This in brief is the skeleton of London's general work language.

London railway terms

To illustrate more fully just one sector of work language, let us take the railways. During the last war, on short leaves before embarking for Normandy with what had been a London regiment of the *Terriers*, I stayed with a Cockney railwayman and his family, all of whom had far more commonsense than I had. For example, one night at the height of the London blitz, as they huddled in fright in the Anderson shelter at the bottom of the garden, I foolishly went out to look at what was dropping. The Cockney, tiny though he was, unceremoniously bundled my great hulk inside again and with good reason, for shortly afterwards the house suffered a direct hit and the family had to be rehoused, from Hackney to Stoke Newington. Even such a short removal within the East End meant a significant change of environment. Stoke Newington houses were larger but more depressing for, although their owners were quite helpful, they lacked the very intimate, friendly atmosphere of Hackney, Stepney, Poplar, Millwall etc.

It was from Cockney railwaymen such as the head of this family that I learnt their great love of special railway words. Not so much the *hail and rain* 'train' type of rhyming slang that the Docklands

Industrial Commercial Development Service is now fond of advertising, but straightforward nicknames. Since British Rail has more than its share of older employees they are still a well-remembered set of words, though after drastic changes to the railway system like Lord Beeching's 'axe' of the 1960s the need to use them has often gone.

Trains quickly acquired non-official names. The Master Cutler to Sheffield was familiarly the *Knife 'n' Fork*; the Royal Mail the *Money Box*; and the Oxford and Cambridge service, long since closed, the *Brains Trust* after the wartime radio programme featuring Professor Joad, Commander Campbell and co. The Wolverton to Willesden parcels train was the *'Orse n' Cart* because it used to have horse-boxes as well as carriages. The *Nelson* was the London-to-Portsmouth train which had only one clear window at the front, the other bearing the name of its destination. Nelson, of course, like this train, was blind in one eye. A high-capacity train working on Southern Region was the *Queen of Sheba*. Although the Biblical queen is described as having a 'great train', her London-area namesake received its title not from its length but from its power.

We may shake our heads at some of these nicknames, but at least they are less confusing than some efforts of official rail language. A certain railway labelled some compartments NO SMOKING ALLOWED until it was pointed out that this allowed passengers not to smoke but did not prohibit them from smoking.

Many of the railway nicknames have had a long life. *The Maze* is Clapham Junction, which was the most intensive railway junction in the world. *Fun City* is Bletchley, a town based on a railway shed and marshalling yard. *Plywood Sidings* were the Thames Board sidings near Barking, Essex, and *Bwani Junction* seems very appropriate for Southall Station since it is used by so many Indians and Pakistanis, and the British railwayman cannot tell which is which.

To relieve the monotony, the old Cockney railwayman sprays into his language plenty of other slang. Thus the *bowlin' green* is the 'fast' line, kept for very smooth-running expresses, overtime is *the land of plenty* or *grab*, a shunter is a *'ooker*, and any tunnel is a *'ole*. Catch-points are *jacks*, plate-layers are *packers*, and *to weasel* is to carry luggage in the hope of getting one of those very useful animals, a *weasel* or tip.

Naturally some of the old names for grades and occupations have disappeared with modern changes. For instance, on the *oxo cube* 'tube' the *weasler* or *porter* has changed into the less descriptive *stationman* through the amalgamation of grades, although one may still meet *live wires* 'underground electricians on maintenance work' *metrognomes* 'drivers on the Metropolitan Line', and *earthworms* or *sewer rats*, a general term for all drivers on underground lines.

Returning to what many consider the railway proper, the question of going 'up' or 'down' by rail is a simple matter of railway politics, dominated by the Cockney railwayman. On all our railways you go *up to* or *dahn from Lunnon* with the exception of the original Midland line, whose offices were at Derby and because of which you go up or down to Derby. With cross-country lines the *up* or *dahn* depends upon which is the direction for reaching central London.

Places

London has an interesting and often amusing collection of place-names. London itself is the *Ol' Smoke*, reminiscent of *Auld Reekie* for Edinburgh although the Clean Air Acts should have dispelled the image of the capital shrouded in *pea-soupers*, dense smogs which used to envelop the city as late as the 1960s.

The Ci'y to a Londoner can mean only his city, and specifically the historical City of London including the *Tahr* 'Tower', *Billingsgit* and the financial quarter. Similarly to a Whitechapel resident *dahn the Lane* refers to Petticoat Lane (home of the famous Sunday market and now re-named Middlesex Street), *up the Row* applies to Club Row and the *Market* to Watney Lane market. *Blood Alley* refers to a place off Whitechapel High Street where sheep used to be killed. *The 'Ighway* would mean Wapping Highway, along which Dick Turpin is supposed to have ridden. South of the river *dahn the Cut* means down Lambeth Walk, and *goin' up the Walworth* meant going along Walworth Road, the main road in Bermondsey. Going *on the Island* refers to the nearest important one, namely the Isle of Dogs. To a fellow-citizen, you do not keep explaining the obvious.

Short familiar nicknames for places are popular. Thus Cockneys who use the garishly painted building at the corner of Dale Street and Hanbury Street, Stepney, do not refer to the Montefiori

Community Education Centre: they speak happily of *de Monty*. *Mud Island* is more correctly *Sahfend* (Southend), beloved resort of many a Cockney and his family.

Many of these nicknames sound facetious. The *'Oly Ci'y* is St Albans. Seething Lane, base of the nearest tax inspectorate, was to dockers *Feevin'* (Thieving) *Lane*. *Saudi* (South) *Kensington* shows the influence of oil-rich Arabs. Whitechapel Road on Saturday afternoon on the Jewish Sabbath, where boys and *gels* would parade, stare and whistle after one another in long-accepted tradition, was one of several *monkey-walks*.

Because of its Australian colony, Earls Court in SW5 is nicknamed *Kangaroo Alley*, though actually many nationalities live there; whilst in Soho lies *Chinatahn*, a small district where almost every shop or restaurant is Chinese-owned. The *White City* is the area near Shepherds Bush where in May 1908 was erected the Great Exhibition, with buildings which were predominantly white. Alexandra Palace, origin of the first London TV transmissions as long ago as 1936, is another former exhibition site known familiarly as the *Ally Pally*.

The Londoner can hardly be expected to say perfectly every place-name that local stalwarts have foisted upon the community. Thus to a Cockney Plaistow is *Plahstow*, Becontree becomes *Beacontree*, and Lenan Street is always *Lemon Street*. Now and then the picture is further confused by folk etymology, where there is genuine belief in a word history which is quite false. The useful magazine *What's On In London*[20] appears to believe that *Piccadilly* was named from people going there to pick daffodils, whereas it was actually named from Piccadilly Hall, a residence of about 1622 of a tailor who made a fortune by selling *piccadillies* (high stiff collars, ruffs, lace edging, etc.), a word from French and Spanish ones meaning 'to prick'. (Compare the Spanish picador who pricks the bull with his lance to weaken it).

Some London road-names are disconcerting. The *Nawf Circular* goes neither true north nor round in a complete circle. And some of the new road-titles are heartless. The *Pearly Way* has become the A23, the *Ol' Kent Road* is merely the A2, Golders Green and St Johns Wood sound less imposing as places 'off the M1'. All London has changed in the telephone system into the mindless monster 01 – the Orwellian horror of it! On the other hand, London still has plenty of rural street names, legacies of the days when places such as Farm Street in the West End, Haymarket, and Saffron Hill near Hatton Garden were in rural areas.

Many London pub-names are most evocative. *Jack the Ripper* naturally stands right in the heart of his murderous territory in Whitechapel. *Charlie Brahn's* in *Lime'ahs* is notorious as the den of sea-dogs and the resting-place till recently of a weird collection of objects: many tourists have enjoyed slumming there.

Pleasanter in association is the *Eliza Doolittle* next to the Shaw Theatre in Euston Road. Round by the old *Jumbo* or *Elephant* (Elephant and Castle) things have greatly changed even in the last few years: old *reg'lars* would hardly recognise the landscape now. In Wapping most of the pubs have had nautical names such as *The Crooked Billet, The Gunboat, The Jolly Sailor* and the famous *Prospect of Whitby*, quite suitably of course because regular sailors lived in nearby streets like Dock Street. Most arresting have been the nicknames e.g. *Sloshers* for a pub in Wapping; and *The Snake Pit* or *Worm* for the Essex Serpent in King Street north of the Strand. Readers might enjoy extending this list.

Other London places have collected nicknames indicating a certain disapproval or disgust, a notorious one being *The Scrubs* 'Wormwood Scrubs prison'. Such also were the *Rookeries* 'Irish ghettoes' and the old cheap lodging-houses like those of Stepney, which included for men *Rahton (Rowton) 'Ahs*, and for women *The Kip*, kept by a Mrs Moss.

However derogatory his own place-names may sound, a Londoner has, it seems, a worse opinion of those in the country. To him *The Sticks* is London's surrounding country area, named apparently from its trees and not the shacks of desultory building, and outside the pale of true civilisation.

High Streets, as in Stepney and Walthamstowe, are named literally from conditions in former days when the main street had to be raised somewhat higher than the ground on each side of it for drainage. Although *streets* are still abundant, the word, stirring images of drab wayfares of tiny terrace houses, is unpopular for new housing developments. Consequently many places looking at first glance just like streets turn out after all to be *closes, avenues, drives, parades*, and so forth. It would be interesting to see what proportion of your friends in London's suburbia actually live in a street. In addition there are some very modern names, like the *precincts* for shopping and the American-sounding *Thames Walkway*.

The place where you can buy that meal sometimes eaten in the street out of a paper bag (the best way to enjoy the taste according to its devotees) is usually the *fish-shop*, though the chips it sells are just as succulent. However, in supposedly better-class London areas it is the *chippy*. Pawnbrokers' shops are practically extinct, but it is not possible to walk far in the East End without meeting a café, pronounced *caff*.

For a public convenience the older Cockney uses the 'rougher' word *lavatory* or *lav*, though that word itself is euphemistic since he does not go there to wash. But for the abbatoir he does use the rougher and plainer term, that being the *slaughter-'ahs*.

In the world of entertainment, pride of place went to the *picture-'ahs* or *picture-palace*. *Goin' to the flicks* two or three times a week was very common, especially for some *kids* and for young lovers wanting to cuddle on the back row; but now the *telly* has killed nearly all those delights. However, a good many Cockneys like going to the *grey'ahnds* (or *dawgs*) and a vast horde love the pub and going to *the match* (there being no need to say which local one it happens to be) to watch teams like Millwall, the dockers' team whose ground was so badly blitzed. Incidentally the London football fan never thinks it absurd that Arsenal, a team historically from Woolwich south of the Thames, should be based well north of it; or that Millwall, seemingly a north-of-the-river team, should have a ground south of it. Being part of London overcomes parochial considerations. Thus place-names from entertainment as well as the workaday world throw another significant light on Cockney.

Directions

Some of these like *straight froo* (through) are fairly standard, others less so. *Nawf, sahf*, east and west are easy enough to follow, and likewise intermediate compass directions even as fine as *nawf-nawf-east*. But only someone like a Thames lighterman would be expected to be conversant with niceties such as *sahf-bi-west*, and even he might not be too sure. 'Diagonally' seems to baffle most Cockneys, the nearest they can usually get to it being to direct you 'straight accraws to de ovver side'.

When guiding *incomers* 'new residents', *furriners* and tourists, Cockneys are in the main remarkably tactful. Nevertheless there is a long-standing joke, of a type prevalent in the Black Country and other supposedly more backward areas of Britain, that they are inclined to provide directions such as: 'Yer can go dahn that alley an' beneaf the tahr-block but it's a bit dicey (complicated) and risky. If I was you, I wouldn't start from 'ere at all, I'd start from Sn' Paul's'. Except on the stage, such perverseness has fortunately still to be met. One of my informants was himself a most experienced London guide, and he ought to know.

Whereas provincials have considerable difficulty wondering whether they go *up* or *down* to London, in view of their positions on the map and London's claims to superior status, Londoners have few such problems. They can clearly go *dahn* south to places like Brighton, they might even go *dahn* to smaller places north of their homes like Luton, and all difficulty can be avoided by travelling simply *to* Manchester, Cardiff, Edinburgh, etc. without stirring North-versus-South hatred or national enmity. A possible conflict of interest exists with Cockneys exiled in the North who remain convinced that their birthplace ranks higher, but imagining a map they generally talk of going *dahn 'ome*. Furthermore the great majority of those who have moved north from the capital have been uprooted from London's suburbia and surprisingly few ex-Londoners will admit to being Cockneys so that the problem, at least in Cockney dialect, hardly arises.

Numbers and quantities

Cockney arithmetic is straightforward. *One, two, free* and away you go, through *'levn, firteen* and *firty* up to a *'underd* and a *fahzen*. The figure o is *noffink* – not nil, nought, zero or some other tricky concoction – or else *nix*, from colloquial Dutch and German *nichts*. A Cockney will sense nothing unusual in talking about a *free-bedroom flat* which has to be paid for. University *stoodents*, or more likely their teachers, may be mildly surprised at the plural in *one pahnd one pence* '£1.01p', but this has become normal in England. A measurement like those in *a two-foot ruler* and *'E's over six foot* needs a little explaining, again to quell pedantic objections about grammar. So common are they in workmen's experience and ordinary speech that they have extended to higher-status usage. Yet, for detailed unusual measurements like *free yards, two feet, one-an'-a-'alf inches*, the Cockney sticks to the Standard English formula if not pronunciation.

Understatements like '*Taint 'alf 'ot*, which could be taken literally to mean 'cold' just as well as 'hot', mean simply that he feels *bleedin' 'ot. Plen'y* and *a lo'* stand for a great quantity: there might be *plen'y* of work to do but not *a lo'* of time in which to do it. A *dollop* is a large unmeasured quantity such as a *dollop o' treacle* or a *dollop* of mud on one's shoes. That concludes a brief analysis of Cockney measurements.

Weather

The old London *pea-souper* has happily gone. No longer do its citizens have to don their smog-masks to fight their way to Waterloo or Charing Cross stations against fog rolling off the Thames. Yet extremes of weather have still to be noted in ordinary conversation. It may be *teemin' dahn o' rain* and, if you venture down the garden *pahf*, you step into *pudduz*. On the other hand, in the height of summer London may be suffering a long and serious *dry spell*, *dry time* or *drawt*.

If bad weather is on its way, there may be a *ring* or *circ-u* round the moon. When the weather becomes very cold, *frawst* or *rime* may be expected on the ground, or also in London vocabulary a blend of words for the same thing, namely *rime-frawst*. As with other spheres of language, the visitor learning Cockney must have at hand his phrase-book of weather. Do not be misled by the guarded language of upper-crust West Enders emerging well-clad from a late show with 'It's a little nippy actually now', for the died-in-the-wool East Ender might assess these conditions as 'It's that bleedin' cold, it'd freeze a brass monkey'.

Nature and animals

Few special nature terms are to be expected in such a built-up area as London. However, 'gorse' is sometimes *furze* besides *goss*, *ling* is heather, and the shallow place with stepping stones for crossing a stream can be a *splash*, even though that is exactly what you want to avoid.

Turning to animals, we shall not concern ourselves greatly with those like foxes rarely seen in Greater London, or exotic ones like those at Regent's Park. Taking more ordinary ones, on the streets roams many a *dawg* and there still trots the occasional mounted *copper* on his *'orse* (less often called *'oss*). *Moke* for a donkey, still said by Cockney children at the seaside and by some of their elders, was common in the nineteenth century (Mayhew records 'I had a good moke'). The gardener and the *'lotment*-holder sometimes see the

effects of another animal although not the creature itself – the *mo-u*
'mole'.

But without any doubt the British animal at present exciting
most language controversy is the *moggy*. Whereas in most of
Lancashire, for example, it means any cat, in the west of that
county it apparently means a mouse; whilst in other parts of
England, according to Joseph Wright's *English Dialect Dictionary*
and my helpers, sightings have been reported in the forms of frogs,
spiders, nits and calves. My general impression is that the word can
stand for any loathsome creature, a possible derivation being Old
Norse *magi* 'stomach'.[21] *Moggy* is certainly the London way to say
it – 'There's a long moggy up that alleyway' was one of the
quainter remarks heard about it. Some of my informants add to the
confusion by claiming what I have not met elsewhere, that the
London *moggy* is only a female cat, the only type which can *kit* (or
kitten) *dahn*, i.e. have kittens. If so, could the word be from *Maggie?*
The whole subject has excited newspaper articles, maps of 'moggy
equals mouse' territory, and local radio debates, so that any extra
light that London could throw upon this animal subject would be
helpful.

The *sparrer* is of course the best known London creature, and
from the male bird's chirpiness the Cockney gets his nickname *cock-
sparrer*. An *ah*, or more frequently *eh-oo*, with loss of its final *l*, is the
owl. Insects include the *earlywig* or *airwig* 'earwig', and *emmets* or
pissimires 'ants'. The mounds erected by these busy insects are not
called *pissimire-ioos*, presumably because that would make it too
large a mouthful, but *ant-ioos* 'ant-hills' or *emmets'-castes*, though
this last with its old double plural is also rather a tongue-twister.
The apparently rude *pissimire* appears among the word options
because of the urinous smell of an ant-hill. A larger creature is
the *flittermahs* 'bat', a word of German origin as can be seen by
comparing the opera title *Die Fledermaus*. The snail is normally the
snai-u but occasionally, the *'oddny-dod*.[22] Another creature is the
devil-on-'orseback, thin, black, and about an inch long. It curls up its
tail when irritated. (In the West Country it is known as the *devil's
coachman*.)

Pond creatures retain some interesting old names, probably
because children like to fish there and they, like many pensioners,
are more closely involved in dialect. (A busy working life in a city
office seems to dispel it, at least until old age). Thus round ponds

some Cockney children still enthuse about *effs* or *effits* for newts, *pollywags* for tadpoles, and like their grandparents *tiddlers* for minnows, the small fish they catch in glass jars.

Even London's animal noises seem to have differed from those of Standard English, as if communication from and to animals is via their own brand of Cockney. Cows sometimes *blart* 'moo' and cats *meh-oo* 'miaw'. On the few farms that survived in Greater London till regrettably they were whittled away by urban sprawl, the animals responded to local words. To both cows and horses the farmer's cry was *Cup, cup!*; to hens either *Cuppy, cuppy!*, *Chick, chick!*, *Coop, coop!* or (you've guessed it) *Cluck! cluck!* The last two calls served also to attract ducks, which makes it sound as if the London-area farmer hardly knew the familiar quack of his own ducks. Pigs would greedily appear at the call of *Tig, tig!*, *Chucky, chucky!* or just the rattle of a bucket. Therefore do not judge all Cockneys by their man-about-the-East-End image: some, in connection with nature and animals, use a few very interesting country words.

Abbreviations

Abbreviations, both old and new, play an important role in Cockney language. Some, like *'cos* 'because', *'kyoo* 'Thank you', and politer *'scuse me!* (Excuse me) for the more direct *Mind aht!*, are constantly on people's lips. Place-names are also abbreviated, especially longish ones like *Stoke New(ington)*.

Cockneys are not idiots: they sense what they are doing to the language. One of the acutest of them freely admitted of the shortened words, 'We 'breviate 'em', abbreviating *abbreviate!* They think too of these shortenings like those of rhyming slang as being forced upon them by the rapid tempo of daily life.

Abbreviations like ordinary words have histories. *Cords* for corduroys may seem a modern shortening but in fact it was first met about 1880. Around the same time *po*[23] for a chamber-pot was first recorded, from the pronunciation *pot* in French *pot de chambre*. Other late-nineteenth-century abbreviations are *cauli* for a cauliflower and *tecs* for detectives. Yet older and dating from early in that century is *mac*, short for mackintosh, the raincoat patented by the gentleman of that name. *'Scuse me*, mentioned above, dates back longer still, about 400 years.

Poverty has brought its own abbreviations. Just as *U.B.* 'unemployment benefit' is now an understood term, so in the 1920s and the 'hungry thirties' a Cockney would say 'I'll a' [have] to go to the R.O.', which was the Relief Office where one could apply for help through the supplementary means test. It was often said 'I'll finish up on the U.B.A.' This involved a *visitor* coming to assess what saleable things an applicant had in the house, such as a *wireless* or (with young couples) a newish set of pots and pans.

At the moment, abbreviations both spoken and written litter London and show no sign of decreasing. They fit its atmosphere, which demands that the citizen should quickly understand one thing and then move rapidly to another. Thus on Liverpool Street Station will be seen cages of BRUTES – a shortening is always better remembered if its initials form a real word – nicknamed from British Rail Universal Trolley Equipment. Another fertile source of abbreviations are the Unions. Despite the sometimes awkward consequences of their actions, for employer and employee alike, names like the N.U.R., N.A.L.G.O., or the N.U.M. sound less hostile as shortenings easily bandied about on the lips of the suffering public.

Technically, such abbreviations are formed in different ways, notably by chopping off the starts of words (e.g. *levn* 'eleven'), occasionally by losing the end of the first word and the start of the next (e.g. the London Stock Exchange use of *Chunnel* for Channel Tunnel shares) and most often by destroying a word's latter part (e.g. *caff* for cafeteria).

Here is a short miscellaneous list, not limited to Cockney areas but very frequent there:

baccy tobacco

B.O. (body odour, from advertisements warning against it)

cuppa cup of tea

fridge refrigerator

G.P. general practitioner, corresponding to the older *family doctor* or still older *panel doctor*

K.O. (i) knock-out (ii) kick-off

lastic elastic

lection election

prentice apprentice

proms promenade music concerts at the Albert Hall

sizes assizes

specs spectacles

S.R.N. state registered nurse

sylum asylum, mental hospital

tayter potato

tice entice

T.V. television

w.c. *water-closet*, toilet. The context and its small-case letters ensure that it cannot be confused with the London district W.C.

Some of those reduced to initials, such as B.O. and K.O. in its knock-out meaning, are euphemistic in seeking to sugar an unpleasant notion – no Cockney wants to be accused of *bad bref* or to be taunted with having been knocked out in a *scrap*. The examples above are only a start. Any walk through the East End, looking at advertisements and hoardings, and listening to conversations, will quickly reveal many more.

Clock and other times

You may hear, "'*E went 'smornin'* (this morning) or '*I'll come 's afternoon* (this afternoon). 'Ago' is dialectal *back* – e.g. *a li(tt)le while back.* '*Alf free* is 'half-past three', '*alf' levn* 'half-past eleven', etc., so that this '*alf* does not mean, as some strangers might think, half way towards the next hour. All this should cause few problems.

However, the Continental 24-hour day is foreign to Cockney. Elderly women especially, at East End transport termini, are inclined to approach total strangers with appeals to have the time-tables translated. Other things even in the English time-system are alien to Cockney – 'evening', for instance. The Cockney has no evening. You may see the word written on church notice-boards, etc. but, if he wants to meet you between tea-time and going to bed, he will suggest, for example, 'Come rahnd to de pub just on eight tonight'.

The first day of the week tends to be Sunday to many church-goers but Monday to those who go out to work. People who belong to both categories generally plump for Monday. *See yer Friday* means 'I shall see you on Friday of this week', whereas *Friday week* or *next Friday* means a week later.

When a Cockney says that he will come *nah*, he means immediately or almost at once. Living in a bustling city, he has to be prompter than, say, the Devon rustic whose *Oi be comin' d'rectly* means that he intends to come fairly soon. Rightly or wrongly, the Cockney prides himself on being a step ahead of his country cousins and, at least in time language, is fairly easy to understand. For that he deserves due credit.

4
Ordinary Slang

Cockney is full of slang, which consists of words used in a joking, rather flippant way. Although the history of the word *slang* is obscure, there may have been an Anglo-Saxon verb *slingan* meaning 'to creep, wind, twist' with a past tense *slang* and a past participle *slungen*[24]; and certainly slang is slung around the East End every minute of the day. The characteristic vocabulary of Cockney is said to be slang.

Slang, which is a matter of vocabulary, is generally thought of as the mass of rather free-and-easy words being used. However some of my helpers think of each separate slangy word as a slang, judging by their remarks about what they call, e.g. 'these kind of slangs' or 'all them slangs'. As usual with slang, most Cockney examples are names of visible things because these are the simplest ideas to grasp.

Slang by its very nature is particularly difficult for outsiders to understand. It changes rapidly, which makes it even harder to follow. Some terms, like *bamboozle*, *bully*, *jazz*, *jeep* and *mob*, have been exalted from its ranks into Standard English, but much of it rises and disappears fairly quickly to be replaced by newer slang. Good examples of this process are all the terms for 'excellent', such as *A1*, *fab* (short for 'fabulous'), *fine*, *grand*, *great*, *kiff*, *posh* (from 'Port Outward Starboard Home', the best way to book cabins on the old luxury liners steaming off S.E. Africa), *ripping*, *super*, *swell* (from the USA) and *yum-yum*. Well-educated Londoners have had their own varieties, such as *first-rate*, *tip-top* and *top-hole*. Recently amongst children *bazzin'* has been in vogue, whilst *smashin'* remains popular, but replacements will soon appear because the slang world is always trying to outdo its previous selections.

All slang has a history – often quite short but sometimes long. Space forbids presenting more than a good spread of Cockney examples with their meanings, but for a closer scrutiny slang dictionaries should be consulted, particularly Eric Partridge's *Dictionary of Slang and Unconventional English* and his *Dictionary of Historical Slang* (see Bibliography).

To start, let us examine orthodox Cockney slang in contrast with the rhyming slang, back slang and other curious types to be dealt with later. This first type, which is by far the commonest, could be called ordinary slang, provided it is realised that what is ordinary to its practitioners may sound quite extraordinary and sometimes repulsive to tourists, 'very genteel folk' and others unused to it.

As mentioned, it undergoes constant change. In 1851 Henry Mayhew in *London Labour and the London Poor*[25] described cant as 'the slang of the patterer'. He pointed out that in London markets you would expect to hear unusual words from stallholders as they tried to sell their goods. They might be expounding the virtues of *crabshells* 'shoes' (from *crabs* 'feet' because they might walk like crabs) or of *sticky*, which was wax. They might mention *cribs* on the *main drag* 'houses in the main street' or a *doxy* 'wife'; or if incensed refer to a *hag-bag* 'woman' or a *flam* 'lie'. They might ask their assistants to bring a *shant of gatter* 'pot of beer'. A quart pot was actually a *cat*, and those for pints and half-pints were *kittens*. To *bilk* was to cheat, a *flyer* a shoe soled without having been welted, and *barrikin* high-flown language as in a remark about the speech of the rich, 'We can't tumble to (understand) that barrikin'. Nowadays one could be excused for confusing *barrikin* with the shouts of angry soccer fans or of theatre-goers having to sit through a woefully inept performance. Apart from *hag-bag*, reduced as in 'She's an ol' bag', such older London slang means little today.

By the time of Dickens a change is apparent. Besides words now unused like *cad* 'bus conductor' and *lush* 'to drink', Dickens employs much slang that is still current, such as *groggy* 'weak, unsteady', *mug* 'face', *ticker* 'watch' and *whop* 'strike violently'.

Current Cockney slang has arrived in various ways, some quite complicated. For example, as the rhyming slang pages show, 'talk' can be *rabbit 'n' pork*. This can be shortened, e.g. ''E's got plen'y o' rabbit' and then altered by substituting the first half of the children's term *bunny-rabbit* to give ''E's ol' bunny today', i.e. he cannot stop talking. It may appear through shortening an expression from someone's name. Thus 'Use yer Neville's' comes from *Neville's loaf* (*loaf* being slang for 'head') from the name of an East End bakery firm. *Up the Jacob's* (short for *Jacob's ladder*) is used both for those on building sites and the trickier rope ones in dockland that stevedores have to climb. A personal name can even stand for an event. For instance, ''E's 'ad a Greenacre (a spill)' is taken from the name of a stevedore who murdered his wife. In the docks industry it means an upset of cargo in a rope net; or even if someone falls from a rope ladder he will complain, 'I've 'ad a bleedin' greenacre this mornin' up the Jacob's'.

To try to explain every burst of his slang to an ignorant listener would infuriate the most patient Cockney: it just cannot be done. Fortunately he reserves the great bulk of his slang for those who know the slang code. To illustrate again from London's dockland, union leaders will urge their men who normally load container waggons, 'Keep the Cherry Blossom', naming a brand of shoe-polish. Since most shoe-polish is black the whole expression means 'Keep blacking the work, keep it on your black list', i.e. refuse to do it. When one expression takes so much explaining, you can see why Cockney slang is often such a mystery to people not *in de know*.

There have been five main sources of Cockney slang:

1. FROM BOXING   In the 1930s especially, there was professional boxing in every London borough each week-night, so it is hardly surprising that it has occasioned so much London slang. My informants, not chosen for their pugilistic prowess, happened to include both an ex-professional boxer and the family of another. Boxing slang has given: *bread-basket* 'stomach'; *kisser* 'mouth'; *conk*, *snitch* and *boko* 'nose' – *conk* standing especially for a large one and *boko* perhaps coming from *beak* plus *coco(nut)*. It has provided *pins* 'legs', nearly always used of both, as 'Gerrup on yer pins!'; and *knock-aht* 'surprise' as 'When I seen (saw) her in all 'er noo togs (clothes), she were a right knock-aht'. Likewise to boxing can be attributed many of the words for beating, such as *hammer*, *lick*, *paste* and *whack*; and *scrap* for 'to fight', which first appeared in print in *The Daily News* in 1895.

2. FROM THE ARMY   *Blotto* 'drunk', as blotting paper soaks up ink; *buckshee* 'free', a favourite of the British Army in India and Egypt; *come the ol' soldier* 'avoid awkward tasks by feigning illness, etc.'; *Jerry* 'German'; *muck in* 'to share'; *scrounge* 'to steal', developed from its original meaning 'to squeeze'; and *wangle* 'to cunningly arrange', which is possibly connected with *waggle* as when a key is waggled to prise open a jammed lock.

3. FROM NAUTICAL LANGUAGE   Sailors have provided Cockney with less slang than might be expected, in view of the facts that long before the time of Wapping press-gangs the East End had close contact with the sea and that its docks lie surrounded by broad-

speaking districts. Examples: *swing the lead* (also an Army term) 'give a false impression', as a lead-line will record a false depth if prevented from dropping naturally; *rope in* 'to include, usually without consent', as 'Yer not ropin' me in on that'; *shove yer oar in* 'interfere'; *shove awf* plus *sling yer 'ook* 'go away'. Another example is *mate* for 'friend', originally a sailors' word from the mate, second-in-command to the skipper, and used since about 1450.

4. FROM THE LANGUAGE OF THIEVES   This has been a rich hunting-ground of slang users. Here belongs a variety of words for 'to catch, 'to steal' and 'to swindle'. A *copper* tries to *nab* criminals, and in the last war both *Cannin' Tahn* and the St Paul's area *copped it bad in de bombin'*. A shoplifter will try to *nick*, *lift* or *pinch* goods, the last coming from the pinching movement of a pick-pocket's fingers. The confidence trickster plans to *chisel* 'cheat' his victim. 'It's a plant!' an accused person will protest, trying to prove he is innocently carrying stolen goods; and 'What a swiz!', a housewife will observe about some rocketing toy-shop prices just before Christmas. 'It's a try-on', she adds, meaning an attempt to gull the customers. A *nark* is a spy, anything *rum* is strange, and if someone is lucky enough to *save 'is bacon* he has escaped.

Prison slang has contributed directly with e.g. *carpet* for three years in prison and 'Gimme a packet o' snaht (cigarettes). But ordinary thieves' slang is remarkably common. Judging by the great quantities of goods claimed to have 'fallen awf of the back of a lorry', the tailboards of vehicles in East End depots should have much stricter Ministry of Transport tests. If you were guided simply by the number of thieves' words known to the average East Ender, you would think yourself lucky to be talking to him safely between his stretches in the *nick* 'prison'.

5. FROM AMERICA   Hollywood, through its *movies* 'moving, originally silent, pictures' and its *talkies*, has been a great influence. From American slang have come, amongst many other terms: *bunk* 'nonsense' (it was America's Henry Ford who teasingly declared 'History is bunk'); *boy-friend* and *girl-friend* for sweethearts, although these words have also filtered into Standard English; and *wise-guy* for someone with a great opinion of himself. A remark like 'I'm no phoney crook (false villain): that poor sucker (dupe)'s a goner (dead man) unless 'e spills the beans (tells what he knows)', is full of slangy Americanisms which soon became favourites, especially with young Cockneys.

Having considered the chief origins of Cockney slang, let us now see to what it is mostly attached. A good deal naturally concerns money, for without that the Cockney could not exist, and, the less he has, the more important to him it is. 'Money' itself is *dough, kelt, bread* (a newer term) or *lolly*, an attractive word, as if money's sweetness could be sucked as a child sucks a lollipop, but actually from Romany[26]. If you *strike it rich* 'become suddenly wealthy', for example after *comin' up on the pools* 'winning the football pools', you are *righ' in the lolly*.

A *quid*, a word which began about 1688, was formerly a guinea but is now a pound, which is also called a *nicker*. During the last war the big white *fiver* used to be a rare piece of paper money in Cockney hands – the sort that *bookies* might flourish at the *dawgs* and *spivs* selling goods fast from their suitcases might handle, but hardly within the reach of ordinary mortals. Now the smaller fivers are becoming commonplace, and Cockney bank clerks will ask 'Do you want it in fivers or tenners?', as if the humble pound note did not exist. Naturally, having to be understood by all sorts of customers, they ask in respectable English: if they employed Cockney spiv language and could be rashly generous, it might be 'Would yer like two grand (£2,000) in *ponies* (£10 notes) or *monkeys* (£25 ones)?'

The *tosheroon* was a word for the old *two bob* or florin. Previously it had meant a crown piece and a half-crown. Other terms like *bob* for a shilling, *frupny bit* for a threepenny bit and *tanner* for a sixpence officially died out with the advent in 1971 of decimal currency, though *ten bob* (10s) for a 50p piece lives on in some Cockney minds and utterances. There seems a gulf of financial manipulation between the old *two bob* coin and ten new pence. With the Mint situated in East London, possibly some Cockney-born administrators feel a trifle ashamed. *Two bob*, for instance, sounded worthwhile – it was a respectable tip and you could buy much more with it – whereas some *cabbies*, given *10p*, have flung the offending coin into the gutter.

Although money does loom large, a Cockney thinks far more about his bodily states and general health. He is not obsessed by imagined illnesses: his is simply a natural interest in what his body is like, and what it can or cannot do. This is why a vast amount of slang, as well as ordinary words, collects around the body.

Here, then, are some examples of Cockney body slang. To show their great ages, they have been listed in order of their first written appearances, though of course they must have been on people's tongues somewhat earlier still:

about 1550   *gob* 'mouth'
about 1590   *paws* 'hands'
      1638   *clapper* 'tongue', especially of a great chatterer
      1664   *noddle* 'head'
      1690   *peepers* 'eyes'
      1708   *mug* 'face'
      1715   *beak* 'nose', now used also for 'judge' and by East End schoolboys for their headmaster
      1719   *gumption* 'intelligence'
      1720   *gab* 'mouth' (*gob*, see above, is earlier). Compare *gift of the gab*. Anyone with this useful gift can talk well and charm by talking
about 1790   *handle* 'nose'

The list is far from exhaustive. For example, we could add *trotters* 'feet', first written late in the seventeenth century; *kisser* 'mouth'; *block, chump, napper* and *nut* for 'head'; *blinkers* 'eyes', besides *bins* (literally 'binoculars') and rhyming-slang *mince-pies*; and for 'hands' *flippers, or mawlies* because they *mawl* or spoil things. Connected with the eyes are terms like *'ave a dekko* and *'ave a gander* 'take a look'; whilst linked with eye and brain is *all my eye* 'nonsense', first recorded in 1768. Yes, much Cockney body slang is comparatively odd; and a remark like 'Shut yer lahd gob, yer ugly mug!', may be effective but is not too original.

Cockney people have attracted a host of slang terms. Some no longer exist, like the low slang *burerk* for an old lady, possibly from Romany *burk* 'breast'. The *screevers*, a word connected with *scribe* and *scribble*, were pavement artists; and *sunshine runners* were casual newsvendors who would hang about newspaper yards to buy a quire or so of a football or race edition at a discount and then run through the streets with them, selling them before their street-corner rivals had a chance.

A word beginning to die is *knocker* for a Cockney dealer in antiques. Formerly they would drive from door to door in their carts, knocking to collect and buy bric-a-brac. Now few Cockneys know it except to mean 'people what tell lies or press yer dahn (disparage you)'. *Totter* for the rag-and-bone man is also beginning to die; whilst the late nineteenth century *allelujah lass* has become simply a *gel from de Sally (Salvation) Army*. *Toffs* and *swells* for well-dressed members of the upper class have fallen out of favour, just like *tart* in its original general sense of 'girl', used alike of those with strict and very loose morals.

Nevertheless there remains a vast quantity of slang for people. *Geezer* (connected with *guiser* 'masquerader') is immensely popular for a person, normally a rather strange one, although in London it can also refer to a foreman or an employer. Rather similar for its slightly contemptuous tone is *bloke*, perhaps from Dutch *blok* 'a fool'. I for one feel a little edgy to hear, for example, some well-educated Cockney teachers referring to people as *blokes*; but this feeling is possibly a little pedantic, like my barely restrained urge to correct the apostrophes in any Cockney *caff* proclaiming, e.g. 'This weeks menu: chip's, pie's, pea's and banger's'.

Kid is very popular for a child, e.g. 'Oh, give it 'im – 'e's only a kid'. As *de kid* it is also frequent for one's younger brother or sister, e.g. 'I went to de Boat Show wiv de kid'. But a parent exasperated with a child will use something else like 'Nark (stop) it, yer little perisher!'

A *tallyman* was a debt-collector, and people buying goods on hire-purchase get them *on de tally* or *on de never-never* because sometimes they fail to keep up payments and so never own them. *Canteen cahboys* are those who teach others to drive – in the depot canteen! They know all about the Road Traffic Acts and in their apparent knowledge resemble *back-seat drivers* and *canteen lawyers* (equatable with the Army's *barrack-room* ones). Whilst on the subject of *law-r-an' order*, we should mention the *mugger* who *mugs* or robs violently to make a *mug* or fool of any old-age pensioner, etc., he attacks; and the guardian of the law. This last gentleman is a *bobby* or *copper* (both traditional Cockney), *fuzz* (more modern) or *pig* (later still).

The array of slang terms for being foolish, mad or drunk shows how much such unfortunates stand out from their fellows. Fools may be *berks*[27], *prats*, *twits* or *gits*. The last is a word of very strong abuse, as in *Yer daft git!* from a Cockney riding an old *grid* 'bicycle' to a hapless pedestrian who veers off the pavement right into his path. Anyone quite crazy has gone *stone bonkers*. Someone out drinking has *gawn on de razzle*, as a result of which he becomes *dippy* 'slightly drunk' or *blotto*, *plastered*, *sozzled* or *well-oiled*.

Many other slang words portray what people do or what happens to them. Of a plausible, *smooth*, *smarmy* foreman it will be said by one of his underlings "E gives me plen'y of toffee'. Thus *Toffee Taylor* (note too the alliteration, as so often like *Smudger Smif*) was the name of one such dockland foreman. These are just the people to guard against, for they can quite easily decide to *shop yer* (inform against you). Here are a few more expressions linked with people, their moods, activities and calamities:

> *'ave a beef* or *chew the rag* 'have an argument'
> *blew 'er top* '(she) became furious'
> *bounce* 'impudence'. Alternative to *lip*, as in *full o' bounce*
> *chap* 'man'
> *coffin nails* 'cigarettes' (when not *Irish jigs*). E.g. 'Get me five coffin nails'
> *do* in vague threats as *I'll do yer*, which can mean 'I'll overcome/hurt/murder you'
> *done for*, *licked* 'exhausted', e.g. of Cockneys after a long useless tramp in search of work.
> *give 'em de ol' G* 'tell them a lie'
> *go to pot* 'be ruined'. Till the nineteenth century this was literary English
> *Keep yer fas'nin' on!* 'Keep your temper'
> *de lads* 'my friends', alternative for *mi mates*.
> *lip* 'impudence'. E.g. "E gives yer a load o' lip'
> *madam* as in 'Don' come 'ere wiv de ol' madam', i.e. 'Don't put on airs'
> *pop* 'to pawn', by taking things to the *pop-shop*
> *kick the daisies, peg aht, snuff it, go west* 'to die'
> *tittle-tattle* 'chatter' (a reduplicative word, most of it repeated like *hurdy-gurdy*).

House slang includes *up de dancers* 'upstairs' (alternative to *apple an' pears*) and the well-known *Put de wood in de 'ole* 'Close the door' *Come rahnd mi drum* (house) is from knocking on a house door as beating a drum. (Early twentieth-century American salesmen were known as *drummers*.) Another American-tinged word for 'home' used in the East End is *joint*. An amusing example, at least for sound sleepers, is when a caller is told that the person sought not in *Uncle Ned* (bed), the usual Cockney term, but *in de snore*. Clothing slang nurtures, e.g., a *pair o' strides* (trousers) and *I' ironed mi flag* (shirt), whilst other things often worn are *specs* (spectacles). Sustenance provides a variety of choice names. A *murphy*, from the Irish surname, is a potato; *goosegogs* are gooseberries. Beer can be *booze*, or *bevvy*, which in the form *bivvy* was Cockney as long ago as about 1840 and may be from Latin *bibere* 'to drink'. A drinker might ask instead for a *pint o' wallop*, with its last word echoing the sound of the beer splashing down his throat. Food itself is *nosh* or *grub*. The latter used to appear in combinations like *bub and grub*, where the '*bub* (strong) drink' was baptised from the sound of the liquid bubbling down. *Grub* is now generally met in the invitation outside taverns to partake of *pub grub*.

Children invent much new slang, especially words with the childish ending *-y* such as *vaccy* 'evacuee' and *rezzy* 'reservoir'. An adult may compare another to a child by saying *'is bottle's gawn* 'he's very frightened'.

But ultimately the greatest breeding-ground of slang is the workplace. Manual workers *clock in* in the morning and *clock aht* at the end of the working day in great social contrast to the office staff who either sign a book or do not formally report in at all. Members of the same gang get to know each other well, with all their strengths, quirks and failings. Such familiarity brings very familiar language. Thus at work we hear much about articles that are *dud* 'worthless' (perhaps originally from Dutch *dood* 'dead'), *U.S.* (abbreviation for 'unserviceable') or *botched* 'badly mended'. A firm may get a delivery of *duff* (faulty) records or plastic baths, on seeing which the storeman says, 'It's no go (no use). Here's a hell of a to-do (very serious matter). Get on the blower righ' sharp, Charlie, an' give 'em a buzz' (i.e. ring the manufacturers immediately about it). At their jobs many employees use a lot of *elber-grease* (hard work) and dare not *knock awf* (stop) work before time for fear of *gettin' the boot, push, sack* or *their cards* – terms which, however flippant they sound, stand for the serious life-changing act of dismissal.

Rhyming slang (which we shall study next) may stick better in the memory, whilst back slang may be excellent to tease the brain; but the nucleus of much Cockney language, as just illustrated, is the catchy but relatively straightforward orthodox slang.

5
Rhyming Slang

''Ullo, Fred. Come in awf of de frog an' toad (road) an' 'ave a cuppa Rosie (cup of tea). It's on de Cain an' Abel (table). But wipe yer plates o' meat (feet) 'cos de ol' trouble an' strife (wife)'s just scrubbed de Rory O' More (floor). She's up de apples an' pears (upstairs) 'avin' a bo-peep (sleep). I'm still on de cob an' coal (dole). Get into that lion's lair (chair) and let's chew the fat (have a chat)'.

Such is Cockney rhyming slang and, although it does not usually break out into such splendid profusion, it has quite a long history in London. It seems to have started in the period 1800–1850, and was becoming strongly established by 1851, when Mayhew[28] called it 'the new style of cadgers' cant . . . all done on the rhyming principle'.

Just where did it start? Matthews states that one origin was in the language of beggars but, since they have no pressing desire to meet each other, this can hardly have been the main source. Julian Franklyn[29] maintains that it arose via the secret language of thieves and was then studied by the police. That seems very plausible because *tea-leaves* (thieves) need a language code to baffle eavesdroppers and to catch them the police need to break that code. A third impetus may have come from bricklayers' slang, which Coleman states was 'the most picturesque, involved and unintelligible' of all the rhyming slang he had heard and was similarly used 'to baffle newcomers'. His examples show that he was referring to exactly the type we are discussing: 'Now then, my china plate (mate)'; out with your cherry ripe (pipe), off with your steam packet (jacket) and set your bark and growl (trowel) a-going'; 'More Dublin tricks (bricks)!' 'Give me some fisherman's daughter (water)'; 'He's elephant's trunk (drunk)'. A fourth origin, suggested by Dodson and Saczek, is that it started from gangs of Cockney navvies, the period 1800–1850 being the era of navvy gangs building canals and railways, and was used by them to confuse rival Irish construction gangs. In my view, Cockney

94

rhyming slang seems to have arisen chiefly from the second and fourth causes outlined above, namely navvies' language taken over by thieves.

Rhyming slang is a form of verbal indigestion, quite opposite to the slurrings and shortenings elsewhere in city speech. Its unexpected twists have long puzzled investigators. Mayhew[30] in 1851 records this example from a thief who said it was used to prevent the *flats* (police) understanding: 'Will you have a Jack-surpass of finger-an-thumb (rum) and blow your yard of tripe (pipe) of nosey me knacker (tobacco) with me and the other heaps of coke (blokes)?' Those examples have disappeared, but the type remains vigorous in London.

Costermongers and their *nippers* (originally costermongers' boy helpers) were amongst the earliest users of rhyming slang; but sporting journals, the *penny gaff* and music-hall songs introduced it to a much wider public. The great artist Lupino Lane for years amused audiences with it in his long-running comedy *Me and My Girl* at London's Victoria Palace. Since about 1900 the London stage and the entertainment world have done much to spread it, which can be seen by the number of personalities who have found their way into its terminology.

Such examples are in plentiful supply. You may be warned "'E'll not 'ear yer: 'e's Mutton Jeff (deaf)', naming an early American strip-cartoon character devised by Bud Fischer. In the British power cuts of 1973 you would be told, 'Give us (me) that 'Arry Randle (candle)', naming a music-hall comedian whose career was at its zenith about 1900. If you are at a loose end, the cry may be taken up, 'Where's de Wilky Bards?' from an old music-hall artist rather like George Formby. *'Obson's Choice* 'voice', from the Northern comedy and generally shortened to *'Obson's*, is further theatrical rhyming slang. *Charles James*, or in full *Charles James Fox*, is 'theatre box'; whilst that other *box*, the god presiding over almost every home, is the *Nervo and Knox*. Other entertainment names immortalised in rhyming slang are from the films *Erroll Flynn* and *Gunga Din* 'chin', and from TV *Alan Whickers* (besides *tug an' stickers*) 'knickers'. To be enshrined in Cockney rhyming slang, like *Harry Tate* 'late', *Tom Mix* 'fix', *Naughton and Gold* 'cold' or the Australian actor *Wee Georgie Wood* 'good', must be for a stage personality the summit of lasting fame.

The old boxing fraternity must also have played a good part in using rhyming slang and extending its bounds. Evidence for this lies chiefly in the names used of old pugilists, such as *Jem Mace* 'face', or *Jimmy Wilde* 'glass of mild (beer)' from the old-time champion Welsh boxer.

Rhyming slang is not limited to London. It is found too on the western seaboard of the USA and in Australia. Tramps all over Britain have used it, and other British cities have a few examples of their own rhyming slang. In Carlisle, for instance, is met the countrified *field of wheat* for a street, whilst Liverpool's nautical environment produces *steam tugs* for bugs. If a Manchester shop-assistant in a fluster makes a mistake, an annoyed local customer may ask her 'Where's mi Whalley Range (change)?', naming one of the less salubrious city districts almost unknown to outsiders.

London is certainly the city with most rhyming slang, and the fact that it grew so quickly there supports the belief that London is its ancestral home. This is not to deny that the type could have sprung up independently elsewhere, an argument supported by many of the Australian examples such as *bacon and eggs* 'legs' which are foreign to Cockney.

From London it has extended somewhat. This was particularly true during the Great War, when it was popularised by the Army. Having served much of my time abroad in the last war with a London regiment, I cannot say that this military popularising of Cockney slang applied then to the same extent, although of course examples like *'alf-inch* 'pinch', i.e. steal, and *Scapa* for *Scapa Flow* 'Go!' would from time to time escape from the mouths of my London comrades. In the last war, residence abroad did not prevent outbursts of rhyming slang, but they did not become markedly prominent.

Published lists of Cockney slang have included *Salford docks* for 'socks', as if London were so short of rhyming slang that it had to import some from other cities; but this is not so. In Salford the term is rare; and the London docker himself is more likely to say for it *East India docks*, *Tilb'ry docks* or *Katharine* (rhyming with *fine*) *docks*.

Formerly rhyming slang was very popular amongst East End pub-goers because the usual atmosphere in a typical English pub is light-hearted and flippant like rhyming slang itself. But in present-day London pubs it is much rarer because so many have been modernised and elderly Cockneys, some of whom are very fond of it, feel rather out of place in them, preferring the more homely atmosphere of the old-fashioned ones. Most exponents of rhyming slang use it deliberately, but in the speech of some Cockneys it is so engrained that they do not realise it is a special type of slang, or indeed unusual language at all – to them it is the ordinary word for the object about which they are talking. Sometimes their *trouble an' strife* does not care for it, thinking that like dialect it may harm her children's career prospects; but grandads especially are fond of it, and it fascinates their grand-children.

Furthermore it has spread from the working-class East End to well-educated dwellers in suburbia, who practise it to exercise their brains just as they might eagerly try crossword puzzles. In status they are far removed from the criminals who were amongst the early users of rhyming slang. It has also found its way into 'comics' which enthral many schoolchildren and which through the power of pictures and the written word may well convince them that the slang is well established and worth imitating.

The charge is sometimes brought that rhyming slang, called by some of its speakers *Matteson Lang*, is far too contrived. Be that as it may, its words are not invented by compilers of Cockney dictionaries: they have first to be on people's lips and not even be a particular fad of one speaker. A few of the current terms may have been coined by music-hall comedians, but in very large measure the entertainers turn into professional fun what they have already heard – otherwise their stage conversations would be unrealistic.

Some young Londoners seem wrongly to believe that, although rhyming slang is active in their district, it is a new type and that the older one has completely died. Here they must be thinking of terms like *borassic (lint)* equalling *skint*, penniless, and of other remarks of their own generation. If they were to consider the matter more widely, they would find it an ever-changing mixture of old and new, with some of the old favourites like *plates of meat* and *apples an' pears* as hale and hearty as ever.

The best rhyming slang combines a rhyme with an apt or provacative social description, as: *artful dodger* 'lodger', *'ockey at the 'alt* 'golf', *trouble an' strife* 'wife', *good an' bad* or *sorry an' sad* 'dad', *Gawd (God) forbids* 'kids, children'. After all, some lodgers are a little devious, golf can be tediously slow and few families live in perpetual matrimonial bliss. Similarly social in its implications is *Rosie (Lee)* for 'tea', from the clairvoyant Gipsy Rose Lee, and with its sly dig at ladies who fondly believe everything told them at

sessions over the tea-leaves. Taking an example which spread
during the last war to the armed forces, at officer selection boards
trick cyclists 'psychiatrists', who were quite kindly gentlemen, would
often be inclined to pass or defer decisions on candidates whom
their fellow officers wanted to reject. The *trick cyclists*, who were
often right, gained their name from their selection procedures
(with random association verbal and picture techniques, etc.),
which seemed rather cunning and bizarre to their Army peers
trained normally at Sandhurst.

Although an expression takes on a different meaning when used
as rhyming slang, there is often an amusing link between the
original and the rhyming-slang meanings. Though less apt as
general social commentary than the examples of the previous
paragraph, there are others where the verbal connexion needs no
labouring, e.g.: *Mae West* 'chest', *bell ringers* 'fingers', *tumble dahn the
sink* 'drink', and *total wreck* (for the person who signs it) 'cheque'.

Every orthodox example of rhyming slang has two, and only
two, stressed syllables. E.g. *Jém Máce* 'face'; *pót an' pán* 'old man',
i.e. husband; *dáisy roóts* 'boots'. Between and around the two
stressed syllables there may be one or more unstressed ones, e.g.
potáto píllin' 'shilling', *dáy's a-dáwnin'* 'morning', *élephant's trúnk*
'drunk', *díg in the gráve* 'shave', *Lancashire lasses* 'glasses'. No
Cockney seriously thinks of it as written above, like a piece of
poetry for scansion; but that is in effect what happens. As he utters
each snatch of rhyming slang he feels subconsciously, as it pushes to
escape, the tug of the vital two stressed syllables conveying the
heart of the meaning.

Looking back through literary history you will find that our
earliest minstrels, like those who recited the long Anglo-Saxon
heroic poem *Beowulf*, remembered their lines through stress and
alliteration, not rhyme. This method continued into the Middle
Ages, for example in the north-western romance *Sir Gawayne and
the Green Knight* and the anonymous poem *The Blacksmiths*, about
those village craftsmen who gave a neighbour many sleepless
nights and which starts:

'Six swarthy smiths besmattered with smoke
Drive me to death with din of their dints (blows).
Such noise on nights heard no-one never . . .'

But it was supplanted by the poetic device of rhyme, a much better memory aid. Cockney slang of the type we are now considering falls into the general modern pattern by depending on stress and especially rhyme. Its rhyme is almost everything.

However, some of the so-called rhyming slang does not rhyme at all. One instance is *Jack Jones* 'alone' (sometimes shortened to *on 'is Jack* 'on his own'), where the gratuitous *-s* is treated like a plural ending as in *bones* or *stones*. A case of what poetry critics call imperfect rhyme is *nanny-goatin'* for 'courting', because *nanny-goat* and *court* do not quite rhyme even in Cockney. (Compare, however, 'coat', which is another meaning for nannygoat in Cockney slang and a correct rhyme). *Bronze figures* for kippers and *rahnd de 'ahses* 'trousers' are other imperfect rhymes.

Yet some of the apparently imperfect rhymes do rhyme to a Cockney. The nineteenth-century *Charing Craws* 'horse' was sounded with the same *aw* that is needed in the nursery rhyme 'Ride-a-cock horse, to Banbury Cross' – a pronunciation normal in Cockney and with older Standard English speakers. 'I'll 'ave a roast joint (pint)' rhymes on the Cockney *I*-sound, which is about half-way between Standard English *I* and *oi*. An impeccable Cockney rhyme, though it may offend purists of speech, is *burnt cinders* 'windows'; whilst *fairy snuff* 'fair enough' is certainly a true rhyme despite its extra *s*.

Some rhyming slang involves a different pronunciation which is more historical than it appears. *Berk* for a fool is from *Berkshire hunt* for 'c—'. *Bark*, like that of a dog, might have been expected; but alternation between the sounds *er* and *ar* is shown by old spellings, present-day Cockney *er* pronunciations in *Derby* and *clerk*, and conversely the old pronunciations *sarmon* for sermon and *varmint* for vermin. Some other twists of pronunciation to suit the rhyme are more dictatorial. The *Dook of York* 'fork' keeps its last sounds, but a film star has his name ruthlessly shortened to provide *Micky Roon* 'spoon'.

Alternatives are allowed. Don't be too surprised if the gentleman standing next to you in an East End pub asks for a *Charlie Freer* when most of the other customers are demanding *pig's ear* or it's shortening *pig's*. Beer can also be called *Crimea, far an' near, Oh, my dear!, never fear, red steer*, etc. Similarly 'gin' need not always be *Vera Lynn* (after the World War II forces' sweetheart), it may be *needle an' pin*; whilst for 'belly' you have the politer choices *pot o' jelly, Auntie Nelly* and *Derby Kell(y)*. The last term comes from two founder members of the Plymouth Brethren in the early nineteenth century, although how the working-class originators of rhyming slang came to know the names of two otherwise obscure middle-class men remains a mystery.

'Arse' may be from late-nineteenth-century usage *Khyber Pass*, or *bottle an' glass*, or with an extra syllable making it an imperfect rhyme *Elephant an' Castle*. Of these choices, the second is preferred, presumably because the extra last syllable of *Elephant an' Castle* weakens its effect. By contrast, no query centres upon 'arse-hole', which is unreservedly and in orthodox fashion *Nawf Pole*.

Different meanings may attach to the same expression, as with *Irish jig*, which can stand for both '*cig*, cigarette' and 'wig'. But the context makes all clear. If, say, you are talking about one used in court by an inky *smudge* 'judge', you will know he is not going to smoke there and perhaps set himself on fire.

Now comes a curious problem. Since *mince pies* are eyes, what are mince pies? If *pig's ear* is what a Cockney chooses to call beer, what does he call a real pig's ear? The solution is that mince pies and without doubt pigs' ears have to be referred to so rarely that, unless someone is feeling extraordinarily witty, they can safely be given their usual names.

When fanatics of rhyming slang are talking, their conversation can be full of it. One of them might say, 'I got up, put on mi east an' west (vest), fleas an' ants (pants), *Dicky Dirt* (shirt), *fourth of July* (tie) an' mi best whistle an' flute (suit). I 'ad a *dig in the grave* (shave) and went dahn the *apples an' pears* (stairs), grabbed some *needle an' thread* (bread) and *bended knees* (cheese). Then I left the ol' *cat an' mahs* (house) and went up the *frog an' toad* (road) to catch the *swear an' cuss* (bus)'. The enjoyment of listening to rhyming slang lies in quickly grasping the clues, as with an entertaining crossword puzzle. You certainly have to be quick and witty to use and appreciate it.

Even where the rhyming slang expression is more than a word long, it may still be several stages removed from the original. A Cockney may complain that he is short of *cod's roe* 'dough', i.e. money. He may remark that his *mate* (friend) is *Brahms an' Lizst*, naming two famous music composers but meaning simply *pissed*, i.e. drunk; or that he is *King Dick* 'thick', i.e. stupid. A newish term in the London area is *borassic*, short for *borassic lint*, equalling 'skint', i.e. 'penniless' (three moves). "'E's in Joe Gurr' = . . . *in stir = in porridge* = *in prison* (three moves again). A still longer one, needing four moves to reach the translation, is *Susy* as in 'Gor a Susy on yer?', from *Susy Anna* = *tanner* = sixpence = $2\frac{1}{2}$ new pence.

This language takes some unravelling, and thus you might be excused for thinking that the London Cockney who uses it is the cleverest city-dweller of all. However, you may be glad to be reminded that rhyming slang is saved chiefly for very informal occasions, e.g. with very close friends on the streets and in the pubs. Luckily, if you ask your way in London, even the most enthusiastic Cockney will not direct you in rhyming slang. And this is just as well, for ordinary Cockney talk can itself be quite hard to follow.

The vocabulary of rhyming slang, as you will be noticing, is concocted from many ingredients. Foremost among these are names of real or fictitious people, such as *Lord Lovel* 'shovel', *Charlie Frisky* 'whisky', *Jimmy Skinner* 'dinner', *Russian Turk* 'work' and *Sammy Wrist* '*pissed*, drunk'.

The connexion in meaning between the names of people and the objects they represent is usually a matter of pure chance. A *Mrs Thatcher* for a *matcher* (an equaliser in soccer) is not her responsibility. The *Dook of York*, so far as we know, had no particular claim to renown through use of or any link with a fork. But the connection through rhyme is clear. No-one doubts why a towel is a *Baden Powell* (the late Chief Scout) or why *Cain an' Abel* are a table; or why strangers in London are *Queens Park Rangers*, unless of course he supports that London football team.

Place names also perform a new linguistic task, as *Rotten Row* standing for a blow, and *Blackwall Tunnel* for a funnel. *Tom tit* 'shit', which has been used since late in the nineteenth century, falls into the disreputable category because of its rhyming ability. A few terms embody curious grammar, notably *didn't ought* (equalling Standard English 'should not' or 'ought not') and meaning the drink port. Rhyming slang snatched from nursery rhymes, as *dickery dock* 'clock', *Movver 'Ubbard* 'cupboard' and *free blind mice* 'rice', is yet another kind and one which seems most odd when suddenly ejected into adult conversation. Comparable to the wealth of ordinary slang for parts of the body and clothing, there is also plenty of the rhyming kind, such as *'alf an' 'alf* 'scarf', *Dover boat* 'coat', *I suppose* 'nose', and the quaintly Scottish sounding *fife an' drum* for *bum*, posterior. Let us now examine some groups of rhyming slang in more detail.

People clothed in rhyming slang often seem excruciatingly funny. The family includes the *bahf bun* 'son'; *bricks an' mortar* 'daughter'; *baker's dozen* 'cousin'; *pot an' pan* 'old man', i.e. husband; *trouble an' strife* or *fork an' knife* 'wife'; *gooseberry puddin* 'old woman', i.e. again 'wife'; *skin an' blister* 'sister'; *slide an' sluther (slip)* 'brother'; *good an' bad* or *sorry an' sad* 'dad'; *one anovver* 'mother'; and the *Gawd forbids* or *saucepan lids* for *kids*, children.

The Cockney underworld brings out its *tea leaves* 'thieves', *Joe 'Ooks* or *babblin' brooks* 'crooks, criminals' and *Bernard Dillons* 'villains' in never-ending battle against the *grass'oppers* 'coppers, police' who have little chance to *earwig* '*twig*, understand' their carefully laid plans. In their ranks will be some people of other backgrounds – e.g. a *board an' plank* or *'am shank* 'Yank', someone out of the *soup an' gravy* 'Navy', or a *four-by-two* 'Jew' (from the cloth pull-through used to clean a rifle). Nor will they all seem men: there will be an occasional member of the female sex in the shape of a *Pall Mall* (in line with the pronunciation *gal*) or a *twist an' twirl*; and an *iron 'oof* 'poof', homosexual'.

People of course have their peculiarities. Some from their unwashed appearance clearly hate the *Cape of Good Hope* 'soap'. Others are for ever complaining, e.g. with 'Enni' (Isn't it) tayters in the mould (cold)?' and at the slightest chance will *go on the Pat an' Mick* 'sick'. Some like *tea-pot liddin' '*kiddin*, teasing' whilst others of an opposite disposition say not a *Richard III* or *dicky bird* 'word', almost as if they were *curran' bread* 'dead'. They do need a lot of attention.

Army service does not destroy rhyming slang. During the last war a battalion of the Devonshire Regiment serving in Burma was composed almost equally of Devon men and Londoners, so the *Japs* quickly became known as *Five-Star Naps*. This came from London's old *Star* newspaper, which gave daily racing tips. Stars were given according to a horse's or dog's chance of winning that day: hence five stars was supposed to indicate a near-certainty. Actually some semi-professionals made good use of the *Star's* forecasts but in a perverse and opposite way, believing that it was nearly always wrong. This allowed them to reduce the list of possible winners for any race, but especially at the *dogs*, by one. One wonders how many punters employ a similar system today.

So much for names of people. There remain many other fascinating groups of rhyming slang, which for convenience and to give a more comprehensive picture now follow in lists and diagrams.

Food and Drink

borrow an' beg 'egg'

bronze figures, Jack the Rippers 'kippers'

gay an' frisky, Charlie Frisky 'whisky' (it does make you frisky)

fisherman's daughter 'water'

Jimmy Skinner 'dinner'

Jimmy Wilde (Welsh boxer) 'mild (beer)'

Joe Blake 'cake'

jockeys' whips 'chips'

loop the loop 'soup'

needle an' thread 'bread'

Robinson Hares 'pears'

ship in full sail 'pint of ale'

squaw an' chief 'roast beef'

stand at ease, bended knees 'cheese'

through my fault 'salt'

tiddlywink 'drink' (hence *tiddly* 'drunk')

Tom Thumb 'rum'

Tommy Tucker 'supper'

you an' me, Rosie Lee 'tea'

Equipment, etc.

April Fools (Aprils) 'tools'

Aunt Maria 'fire'

baa-lamb 'tram'

Baden-Powell, bark an' growl 'towel'

burnt cinders 'windows'

Cain an' Abel 'table'

Cape of Good Hope, Bob Hope (American comic),

Band of Hope 'soap' (even though this teetotal organisation started in Manchester)

Charles James Fox 'box'

cherry ripe 'pipe'

Dublin tricks 'bricks' (influence of Irish navvy slang)

Dook of York 'fork'

jackdaw an' rook 'book'

jam jar 'motor- or tram-car'

Joanna 'piano'

Lancashire lasses 'glasses, spectacles'

Lill Lane 'train'

Johnny Randle, 'Arry 'Andle 'candle'

linen draper 'paper'

lion's lair 'chair'

Lord Lovel 'shovel'

Micky Roon 'spoon'

Molly Malone 'phone'

oily rag, Harry Wrag '*fag* cigarette'

oxo cube, 'tube, London underground'

pen an' ink 'sink'

rollin' biller, weepin' willer 'pillow'

Rory O'Moore (Irish influence again) 'door' and 'floor'

twos an' threes 'keys'

Uncle Ned 'bed'

Wilkie Bards 'playing-cards'

Places

Albert 'All 'wall'

battle-cruiser *'boozer*, public-house'

dolly mixtures *'pictures*, cinema'. E.g. 'See yer ahtside the dolly mixtures'

Eastern foam 'home'

flowery dell 'prison cell' (euphemistic)

frog an' toad 'road'

Noah's Ark 'park' (where many of the animals walk two by two)

tidy an' neat 'street'

whale an' gale 'out of jail'

Money, etc.

bees an' 'oney 'money'

I'm goin' to the *cab rank* (bank)

on the *cob an' coal, Ol' King Cole* (dole)

cod's roe *'dough*, money'

Duke of Kent 'rent'

greengages, 'wages'

Gregory Peck, total wreck 'cheque'

Lady Godiva *'fiver*, £5 note'

rock of ages 'wages' (all depends on it)

saucepan lid *'quid*, £1'. A customer whose turn it was to pay for drinks went outside the pub for a moment, returned with one of these large and heavy objects, and astonished the barman by banging it down on the counter with the request, "ere, take it aht o' that'.

sausage an' mash 'cash'

tayter pillin' 'shilling'

Miscellaneous

Adam an' Eve 'believe'

alligator 'later'. Cf, the trick saying, 'See yer later, alligater'

cock linnet, 'minute'

bull an' cow 'row, argument'

Have a *laugh an' joke* (smoke)

pen and ink, 'stink'

plates an' dishes 'misses' (imperfect rhyme)

stick of chalk 'walk'

Tom foolery, 'jewellery'

top 'at, brahn 'at 'cat'

Shortenings

What makes it even harder to follow is that some rhyming slang is shortened. This is no new development, for written records show that abbreviations have been used in Cockney rhyming slang for over 120 years. In 1859 J.C. Hotten in his *Dictionary of Modern Slang, Cant and Vulgar Words*, instanced *Nose-my* shortened from the *Nosey-me-knacker* 'tobacco' that appears e.g. in Mayhew's book. Nowadays a Cockney will not go to the trouble of saying that his

The Body

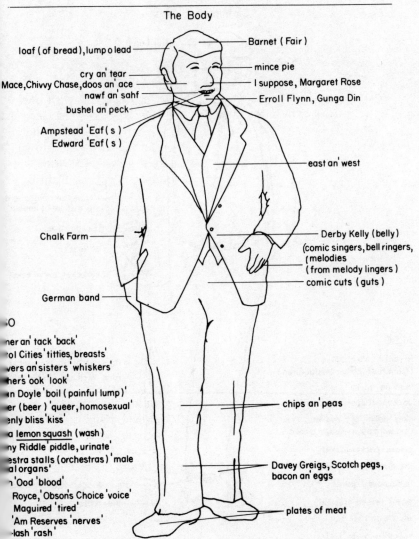

loaf (of bread), lump o lead

Barnet (Fair)

mince pie

cry an' tear

Mace, Chivvy Chase, doos an' ace

I suppose, Margaret Rose

nawf an' sahf

Erroll Flynn, Gunga Din

bushel an' peck

Ampstead 'Eaf (s)

Edward 'Eaf (s)

east an' west

Chalk Farm

Derby Kelly (belly)
(comic singers, bell ringers,
(melodies
(from melody lingers)
comic cuts (guts)

German band

O

...ner an' tack 'back'
...ol Cities 'titties, breasts'
...vers an' sisters 'whiskers'
...her's 'ook 'look'
...n Doyle 'boil (painful lump)'
...er (beer) 'queer, homosexual'
...enly bliss 'kiss'
...a lemon squash (wash)
...ny Riddle 'piddle, urinate'
...estra stalls (orchestras) 'male
...al organs'
...n 'Ood 'blood'
...Royce, 'Obson's Choice 'voice'
...Maguired 'tired'
...'Am Reserves 'nerves'
...lash 'rash'

chips an' peas

Davey Greigs, Scotch pegs,
bacon an' eggs

plates of meat

friend is *elephant's trunk* 'drunk', he's just *elephants*. He no longer takes a *butcher's 'ook* 'look', just a *butcher's*. He puts on his *daisies* and *titfer*, short for *daisy roots* 'boots' and *tit fer tat* 'hat'.

Shortened rhyming slang arises from a need for economy. By its very nature, though it is often amusing, rhyming slang is

Clothes

titfer (tat)

'alf a dollar

Peckham Rye

Dover boat, all afloat, isle afloat (coat)

Epsom races

Dicky Dirt

Sky rocket, Lucy Locket

rahnd de 'ahses (trousers)
rank an' riches (breeches)

almond rocks, Katharine Doc

daisy roots

ALSO

Bryant an' Mays 'stays'
(from the match manufactures)

Irish jig 'wig'

Jack the Ripper 'slippers'

okey-doke 'poke, pocket'
(old word as in 'a pig in a poke')

steam-packet 'jacket'

these an' those 'clothes'

turtle doves 'gloves'

watercressed 'dressed'

whistle an' flute 'suit'

Yorkshire blues 'shoes'

unnecessarily long; and there is really no need to use two or three words like *whistle an' flute* 'suit' where just one such as *whistle* will do. The spread of industry has also helped to destroy some of the longer expressions. There is no time at work to shout e.g. 'Shut yer box of toys (noise)!': 'Shut yer box!' is enough.

When two Cockneys are conversant with shortened rhyming slang, one will not offend the other by talking down to him by using the full forms. To *bullock's 'orn* (alternative to the ordinary slang verb *pop*) means 'to pawn', but normally an article is just *bullocked*. Full rhyming slang, however, seems to be preferred when the speaker wants to stress what he is saying.

One or two of the shortenings have quite vulgar meanings. Well-known is the *raspberry* as in 'They blew a raspberry at 'im', but few realise its origin. It is short for *raspberry tart* meaning *fart*, break wind. Another is *pony* for *pony an' trap* 'crap'. A third is *wick* from *'Ampton Wick*, i.e. *prick*, penis. An informant tells me that *gipsy's* for a *gipsy's kiss* 'piss' was used innocently by two of his clergymen friends. If their derivations were more widely known, such terms would become less popular.

But abbreviation is impossible where the two stressed words in the full rhyming slang make a personal name. You cannot shorten, say, *Aunt Maria* 'fire' or *Uncle Willy* 'silly' without mystified hearers wondering what aunt or uncle is being talked about. Here follows a selection of shortened rhyming slang:

almonds 'almond rocks', socks

Aris 'Aristotle', bottle. Also used for 'arse', e.g. "E's go' a right Aris'

Barnet 'Barnet Fair', head of hair. E.g. 'She's go' a nice Barnet'

bird 'bird-lime', time (prisoners' rhyming slang)

butcher's 'butcher's hook', look

mi ol' china 'china plate', mate

daisies 'daisy roots', boots

Dennis 'Dennis Law', policeman (from the Scottish international footballer)

flowery 'flowery dell', prison cell

Germans 'German bands', hands

Grimsbys 'Grimsby docks', socks. E.g. 'Where's mi bleedin' Grimsbys?'

'Ampsteads 'Hampstead Heath', teeth. Sometimes also *'Amstead 'Eafs*, as if it came from a strange double plural *teeths*

'ickery 'dickery dock', watch or clock. E.g. "Ave a butcher's (a look) at this 'ickery'

Jack in *on 'is Jack* from *Jack Jones* 'alone'

minces 'mince pies', eyes

nanny 'nanny-goat', coat
'Obson's 'Hobson's Choice' (play with North Country accents),
    voice. To a Cockney, Northern dialect sounds unusual.
Oxford 'Oxford scholar', dollar
Peckham 'Peckham Rye', tie. E.g. 'That's a lovverly Peckham!'
rabbit 'rabbit an' pork', talk. E.g. 'Don't keep rabbitin' on'.
Scapa! 'Scapa Flow!', Go! (from the Scottish naval base where
    the German fleet was scuttled after the Great War)
Sweeny 'Sweeny Todd' (from the play about the demon barber
    of Fleet Street). Means 'flying-squad' (cf. TV's *Kojak*
    programme)
Thomas Tillin' 'shilling' (from the motor transport firm)
titfer 'tit-for-tat', hat
turtles 'turtle doves', gloves

Here is a recent poem in rhyming slang by Barbara Hoy[31], a
lady who was herself born within the sound of Bow Bells (if the
wind was blowing in the right direction at the time):

UNCLE GEORGE

Mi old Uncle George was a shuvver	shuvver = chauffeur
Gawd! e'd the gift o' the gab,	gift o' the gab = ability to
E'd go on arf the night	express himself
(If 'e wasn't too tight)	tight = drunk
To the geezers 'e drove in 'is cab.	geezers = people
Baht the 'ard-up and ungery firties	
When a bloke ud damn near sell 'is soul	
To any ol' nob	nob = well-off person
What ud give 'im a job	
And save 'im from takin' the dole	
Yer couldn't afford to be choosy,	
Yer'd work till you dropped for a quid	quid = £1
For yer trouble an' strife	trouble an' strife = wife
And to keep bref o' life	
In a blitherin' young saucepan-lid	saucepan-lid = *kid*, child
There wasn't no trips to Majorca	
Wiv good bees an' 'oney to spend	bees an' 'oney = money
Yer'd be livin' it 'igh	
Wiv two bob in yer sky	sky (-rocket) = pocket
On a charrybang bahnd for Sahfend.	charrybang = char-a-banc

If old Uncle could put up for parlement,
E'd stand on 'is plates and e'd shaht,   plates (of meat) = feet
In a voice full o' scorn
'Lads, yer dun-no yer born,
Yer dun-no what 'ardship's abaht.

Nah go an' take a good butcher's   butcher's (hook) = look
At our standard of livin' today;
We've all got a telly,
A full derby kelly –   derby kelly = belly
And we're strikin' the ol' lot away!

Britannia's gawn right up the Swanee,
Wiv closed minces we foller the oafs.   minces (mince pies) = eyes
We're in bad two-an'-eights   two-an'-eights = states
Buckle to, mi ol' mates
And for cryin' aht lahd use yer loafs!'   loafs (of bread) = heads

Bingo rhyming slang

In bingo (older names *lotto* and *'ahsey-'ahsey* from the excited cry *Full 'ahs!*), quick thinking is essential. Not only is it vital to obey general instructions like *eyes dahn* to start the session and *card check*, but to understand rhyming slang. Bingo rhyming slang carries a smaller proportion of people's names than ordinary rhyming slang, but they occur (e.g. *'Arry Tate, Tom Mix*). Research has not yet brought to light a complete set of bingo numbers dependent on rhyming slang, but the list is growing:

    1 = buttered scone
    2 = me an' you (or Dr Who from children's TV)
    3 = you an' me (or up a tree)
    4 = knock at the door (or door to door)
    5 = Jack alive, dead alive
    6 = Tom Mix, (more modern) choppin' sticks or chopsticks
    7 = Gawd's in 'eaven
    8 = 'Arry Tate
    10 = cock(s) an' 'en (otherwise Dahnin' Street)
    12 = monkey's cousin 'dozen'
    15 = rugby team (correct for rugby union but imperfect
        rhyme)
    22 = dinky-do

44 = menopause 'all the fours'

66 = clickety-click (imperfect rhyme) or chop(pin')-sticks

In Cockney bingo-halls the other numbers have names derived in all sorts of ways, for example:

9 = 'Orspital or doctor's orders (No rhyme. From no.9 pills formerly given in the Army)

11 = Legs eleven (from the shape)

13 = Unlucky for some

21 = age o' mi ol' dutch (all ladies like to be thought younger)

22 = two ducks (from the shape of the figures)

26 = 'alf a crahn (old money)

30 = speed limit

49 = Cannock-nuff (from Great War attempts at French *quarante-neuf*) or copper (from PC 49 of radio)

65 = Stop work (men's retirement age)

76 = Was she worf it? (from 7/6d., the old price of a marriage licence) or the trombones (from the song about 76 trombones)

77 = Two little crutches (from their shape)

88 = Two fat women (from their shape)

99 = Top of the tree (highest number)

Perhaps in time rhyming slang will be clever enough to conquer all the set.

Front and back slang, and other coded language

Certain other methods are in use, not often but more so in London than elsewhere in Britain, to prevent eavesdroppers understanding a conversation. One device is front slang, whereby the same extra syllable precedes each word. Thus, to warn her *ol' man* of danger to their child about to fall off a parapet, his *ol' china* might say 'Dee-mind dee-that dee-edge' or 'Ger-she'll ger-fall'. They then have a better chance of grasping their toddler before, frightened by their words and sudden movement, she overbalances. In the same way, if their very young boy is about to play with *the lectric*, they will warn each other 'Oo-watch oo-that oo-plug'.

A more difficult system is partial back slang, where the word's first letter is put after the rest of the word and an extra syllable added, so that, adding for instance -*ay*, 'Watch!' sounds like *Otchway!* and 'Go!' like *Ohgay*!

Full back slang is where words are said completely back to front, *yob* 'boy' and *talf* for 'flat (apartment)' being well-known ex- amples. It has long been used for the lower numerals, for in 1851 Mayhew reported[32] that a young pickpocket had told him that he knew *eno* 'one', *owt* 'two', *eerht* 'three', *ruof* 'four', *evif* 'five' and *exis* 'six', but added 'I don't know any higher'. My informants can go higher, though their pronunciations do not tally with those of the nineteenth century, theirs being: *eno* (1); *ow'* with a glottal stop (2); *erf* (3), rhyming with Standard English *turf* and with Cockney *f* for *th*; *roaf* (4), rhyming with *loaf*; *eevif* (5); *exis* (6); *nevis* (7) – note the change of vowel; *eight* (unaltered); *neeno* (9), rhyming with the title of the 'comic' *Beano*; *net* (10), given also last century to Mayhew[33].

Back slang is said to have originated at Billingsgate fish-market; and certainly Billingsgate market porters, besides costermongers, butchers and other local food traders, used it. Mayhew[34] was told it was unintelligible to the Irish inhabitants of London, examples given to him including: *reeb* 'beer', *deb* 'bed', *on doog* 'no good', *nammow* 'woman, i.e. sweetheart', and *tib of occabot* 'bit of tobacco'.

'All a fellow wants to know to sell potatoes', he was told by a master street-seller[35], 'is to tell how many tanners make a bob, and how many yenaps a tanner'. To follow this advice, modern traders will want to know especially what a *yenap* is. It is back slang for a penny, though as with so much back slang it is only a very rough transposition of the letters. Indeed, in changing from *penny*, *yenap* (rhyming with *ten up*!) has grown a letter *a* and an unstressed vowel, and lost one letter *n* and the sound *i*.

Matthews states that, although a few words like *slop*, *traf*, *sip* and *yob* have been general in Cockney at various times, it has usually been restricted to constermongers for trade purposes. He states that the inverted numbers *eno*, *owt* and *erth* (yet another back slang pronunciation for 'three') were sometimes used by East End card- players; but that back slang was still commonest among trades- men, especially butchers and dealers in raw foodstuffs, and that it was in places like Smithfield and Spitalfields that they still used such gibberish as *delo woc* 'old cow'.

This is exactly what I find. Back slang is used most of all in *Billingsgit*, *Smiff-field* and other places where it is often safer to talk over the head of a customer. In the butcher's shop when chopping meat one butcher may remind another, 'Don't forget to charge for the eenobs (bones) an' taf (fat)'. His assistant might ask, 'What's the *eecrip* (price) of the team (meat)?', to be answered 'erf a do-nip (three a pound)'. Again, with words like *eecrip*, *erf* and *do-nip* it is clear that exact back slang, with every letter positioned according to rules, is the exception. For example *slop*, derogatory for a policeman, is an abbreviation of *esclop* 'police', whilst *sip* 'make water' has lost one *s*.

Back slang is still rife at *Billingsgit*. *Doc* for cod was constantly being used there during the last war. *Eeloc* is *'coalie*, coal-fish' and *eethlaps* is plaice (quite a change here!). The fish-merchants will ask each other, 'What's the eecirp (another variation for 'price') of nomlas (salmon)? 'Naturally some fish-names, like that of the gurnard, are hard to back-slang, and others it is unusual to change. For example the monk, called by Midland wholesalers the *angler-fish*, *Scotch 'olibut* or *Nellie*, receives at Billingsgate its normal name. Where they wish, London wholesale fish-merchants will resort to back slang not merely for fish-names, for example 'Ah did Bill get on this mornin'?' "E was flach kenurd (half-drunk)'.

Lightermen also use back slang, but not to prevent others overhearing. If they have to work in darkness more than eight hours, they are doin' a long tidgin (night shift). The gang on the *'apny dip* 'ship' would understand.

In the last Billingsgate example, *flach* 'half' shows the regular back-slang substitution of *ch* for initial *h* because a final *h* in back slang would hardly be noticed. This *ch* was employed in an incident recently observed by a colleague. He heard two Cockney *yobs* on a bus remarking about the violently red hair of the girl in front of them, saying *Kool ta tath riach*! 'Look at that hair!', at which the girl turned round and hit them over the head. What they had been saying was tantamount to whispering about her, but for such an angry reaction she obviously understood it.

The instance of the red-headed girl proves that back slang is not confined to trade uses. If a girl passes in mini-skirts, to draw the attention of his *mate* a man will say, *Ivachy kool elrig gels* 'Have a look at that girl's legs'; and, if the other man likes them, he will respond *Dug*! (Good!). *Dug yed* is a useful greeting for *'Good day!*, i.e. Good morning! *Deeracs* are playing-cards; and time, unless referred to as in 'What's de enemy?', is *eemit*. At the cry *Sree rac*! (besides *Jam-jar*), the waiting Cockney of old would spring into activity, for it meant 'Here's (the) tram-car!' Finance was directly affected too, because a *flach yenork* was a half-crown, and a man could be asked how much *yenam* (money) he had in the *kaynab* (bank).

Back slang has also a polite, or comparatively polite, use. In these days when the Cockney has to be more careful in the presence of women, he may use it to tone down his swearing and uncouth words. Thus *dratsab* or *drabsab* is 'bastard', *sippus* or *sip* is 'piss', *Kakuff it!* is 'F—it!', and a *kukuffin' tunuc* is a 'f—c—'. Even so, and though their original meanings are almost lost, they are not terms it seems necessary to pursue here in the finest detail.

Another use of coded language to defy a possible eavesdropper is by a special metaphor. For example, an ex-docker who is now a security officer at a London college was in the process of phoning his sister when he suddenly asked her, 'Can yer 'ear a drip?' and quickly put down the receiver. At his college he had learnt that, by some clever means, certain overseas students had found a way of making expensive phone calls home without burden on their pockets. He meant 'Is the phone being tapped?'.

To summarise, then, the Cockney has at his disposal a number of ways of bewildering an eavesdropper. They all demand good intelligence, which confirms what is already coming to light, that language portrays its user; and, when he is a Cockney, that usually means someone of agile brain and tongue.

6
Grammar

The Cockney is often accused of having 'no grammar'. What is meant is that his grammar disobeys the rules of Standard English, because every language and every dialect must have its grammar in order to link words and ideas. Without grammar, written and spoken language could have no meaning. Be careful too with another common accusation about Cockney grammar, that it is 'bad'. Where the Cockney needs to use his own variety of English, he is entitled to use its grammar, which far from being 'bad' is the most suitable for that purpose.

The grammar of the London Cockney has never been thoroughly investigated, which is a pity since what strikes some outsiders most is not always the pronunciation or even the special words but the grammar used to connect them. To hear, for example, *It ain't 'im what done it* can take a listener by surprise and distract from what is being said to merely how it is being said. This is important, because in language grammar is supposed to be the surest social marker.

Word order is vital. This is more important in English than in tone languages like Chinese or those like German which depend a great deal on inflexions. In Cockney of course, as in the rest of England, 'The boy kissed the girl' would show that the boy started this interesting action and be quite opposite to 'The girl kissed the boy'. 'The dog bit the postman' records a sporadic London incident, as warnings at *Mahnt Pleasant* sorting office have shown; but 'The postman bit the dog' sounds incredible – Cockney postmen are not so *potty*.

Although Cockney generally obeys rules of Standard English word-order, they may be upset by special emphasis, causing the most important words to come first. E.g.: 'A ree-u (real) beauty i' was'; 'Fair dropped a clanger, 'e did', i.e. he made a great mistake 'Anybody what narks my bird (who annoys my girl-friend), clobber (hit) 'em'. Sometimes the result is that the main verl vanishes but the subject reappears in different wording, as 'A fai' stunner, that drink what yer made', i.e. you made a marvellous drink.

Still considering sentences as a whole before delving into finer details, two general points need stressing. First, there are occasional redundancies like *so derefore* where *so* would be enough; *but 'ahever* (however) we shall accept them as allowable Cockney. Secondly, and far more often, words are omitted. In air raids, when Londoners were dozing in their communal shelters, some wardens using their temporary authority would shout, 'Aht (Put out) that fag!'. Other examples abound: 'Tha' i', love (Is that it, love)?'; 'We 'ave a concert Toosdy (on Tuesday)'; 'That what they (is what they are) called'; 'aht (out at) the back'; 'Ah far yer (are you) goin', gel?'; 'Ah much rent yer (do you) pay?'; 'Oo, cawst yer (it will cost you) a lo' a money'; 'There was a feller rung (who rang) up'.

So far, so good – Cockney grammar's outline has been shown. Next, since every language and dialect seems to have no more than eight basic parts of speech, let us take in order those eight components of Cockney.

Nouns

Cockneys have a fondness for certain compound nouns. These are usually a bit rough and startling, but most vivid and descriptive. For example, unless you watch your step, they may brand you a *know-all*, *bossy-boots*, *clever-britches*, *clack-fart* 'tell-tale' or *flibberty-gibbet* 'flighty person'.

Cockney noun-endings differ little from those of Standard English. A peculiar survival is an additional vowel after *st*, making *postes* 'posts', *nesties* or *nesses* 'nests' as in *robbin' birds' nessies*, and *fistes* 'fists'. It has been used in London since at least 1791, when John Walker's *Pronouncing Dictionary* mentioned it, and has been encountered fairly recently; but it is so rare that you may not hear it. Very common, however, is the unchanged plural after numbers, as: *four foot, three mile, six year since* (ago), *forty pahnd, dis last free week* 'this, i.e. these, last three weeks'. The last type of usage arises from common expressions in workmen's speech. In less frequent measurements, such as *two feet five and a half inches*, Standard English plurals (in this case *feet* and *inches*) have a greater chance of being used. And when the Cockney shopkeeper asks you for, say, *free pahnd one pence*, he puts *penny* into the plural because the price he expects contains a lot of them.

Pronouns

In personal pronouns, the Cockney tends to put the accusative for the subject of a sentence. Thus: 'Me an mi brovver was born 'ere'; 'Im an' 'er's gettin' wed'; 'Me an' 'im's bin great pals'. Notice that, contrary to the practice in Standard English, where the speaker is one of two subjects (like the *Me of Me an' 'im* in the last example), he comes first even though to educated people it sounds less polite. *Us* is often used for 'me' as in 'Give us it!' This has been called the 'plural of modesty', similar to a monarch's use of the royal *we* for 'I', as if others are included in what he wants; but, when anyone shouts, 'Give us it!', it sounds anything but modest.

Yet hyper-correction also occurs when Cockneys who know that they too often say *me* for 'I', try to correct it by putting *I* where it does not belong. Even some educated Cockneys in trying to be careful will do this, stating, e.g. *between you and I* or *I've told you about my brother and I*. One morning, the story goes, a London University professor arrived at his office so early that he heard the Cockney cleaner still at work inside. Not wishing to startle her, he knocked before entering. 'Who's there?' she asked, and when he replied, 'It's me, Professor Smith', she first refused to let him come in, believing that every professor would say, 'It is I'.

For emphasis, an extra personal pronoun may appear, like saying 'he' or 'she' twice. Even if it seems the subject of the sentence, this stressed pronoun goes into the objective case. Thus: "'E's a right layabaht, *'im* '(though *'E* and *'im* are the same person); "*Er*, she wouldn't tell a blind man the time, tell 'im (she would tell him) to look 'isself'.

In relative pronouns, *what* is quite frequent for 'who(m)' and 'which'. For example, "Im what's talkin' (He who is talking)'; 'a chap what I noo (whom I knew)'; "'E're's somefink what (something which)'ll 'elp yer'. But relative *as* is also found – thus 'that noise as (which) you 'eard'. In fact, the frequency of this *as* is shown by the story of the two Cockney bad spellers. One asked his friend, 'Ah d'yer spell *whoddle*?' (meaning to write 'what'll fit'). The other replied, 'That's wrong anyway – it should be *uzzle* (*as'll*)'.

Even where the relative pronoun according to Standard English rules is correctly chosen, the Cockney speaker can forget how he began the statement and get into rather a tangle. For example, 'A chap whose gang was next to mine, 'is gang was awlus laughin' at 'im. . . .'

Along with the need to speak quickly before someone else butts in, confusion over these pronouns may well be the reason why so often they disappear, as for instance from: 'There's a bar goes froo (which goes through)'; "Taint everybody can fix (who can mend) a telly, but there is some does (who do) it'; 'There used to be a boat go (which would go) up the river'.

The possessive pronouns *yourn* 'yours', *hisn* 'his', *hern* 'hers', *ourn* 'ours' and *theirn* 'theirs', which used to be characteristic of East Midland dialects, are sometimes still heard in Cockney. They finish with an -*n* modelled from *mine* and older English *thine*. Examples: 'It's not yourn, it's ourn'; 'That kid(child)'s one o' theirn'. In 1817 such forms were being attacked as 'errors of pronunciation and improper expressions used frequently and chiefly by the inhabitants of London'[36], but in Cockney they are still not quite dead.

The -*self* pronouns can also differ from those of our standard language. The unusual-looking *'isself* and *theirselves* are modelled on *myself* and older English *thyself* because the elements *his*, *their*, *my* and *thy* are all genitives. These pronouns are common in the writings of Dickens and still widespread:

A (As emphatic pronouns, for stress) 'I did it all myself', "E couldn't do it 'isself', 'She told me so 'erself', 'They should try it theirsells (themselves)'.

B (As reflexive pronouns) 'Yer've cut yerself shavin'', "E killed 'isself', 'They sat theirsells (i.e. sat) dahn'.

Other abnormalities amongst these and similar pronouns are *one annover* 'each other', a very rare *yer* as in *Sit yer (i.e. Sit) dahn*, and singular for plural as *Be'ave yerself* (yourselves).

Indefinite pronouns are generally employed as in Standard English, but three are pronounced very differently: *noffink*, *nuppm* 'nothing'; *somefink*, *suppm*, *summat* (literally *somewhat*) 'something'; *anyfink* 'anything'.

Demonstratives include *this* for someone or something not yet pointed out, as 'We went to this show' (without having said which it was). It is a growing and perhaps irritating practice, especially amongst youngsters. *Them* 'those' is very common both as an adjective (*them books*) and standing by itself as a pronoun, e.g. *for them what likes (those who like) doin' it*. *This* is sometimes followed by what seems an unnecessary *'ere* to stress how close or immediate it is, e.g. 'This 'ere (this) feller that I seen'. For pointing to something distant, *yonder* is sometimes still heard, giving, e.g. *that yonder* and *them (those) yonder.*

Verbs

Cockney verbs have a number of striking features. In free conversation all the present tense can finish in *-s*, though the practice is rapidly dying. Thus: 'I/you/he/she/it/we/they goes'; 'They keeps stoppin''; 'I lives in Stepney'; 'You finds a lo''. Analogy causes the frequent use of *is* for plural *are*, and *was* for plural *were*, e.g. 'The fellers is goin' to the dawgs (greyhound-racing stadium)'; 'We was in'; ''Im an 'er was married'; 'They wasn't spotted (weren't seen)'; 'Oh, wasn't they?'.

Sometimes the reverse happens and a plural form is linked with a singular subject, for instance: 'As I were (was) sayin''; ''E weren't 'alf tight!', i.e. he was quite drunk. This last example shows, incidentally, the Cockney quality of understatement as he was actually much more than half *tight*, he was very drunk.

Past tenses and past participles

What strikes many visitors is the number of unorthodox past tenses and past participles. A very teasing question is whether remarks like 'I know 'e done it' contain a genuine past tense, with *done* standing for 'did', or whether just an *s* has dropped out, since 'I know 'e's done it' would have sounded almost normal. But the Cockney seems to think of 'I done it', 'They seen it', etc. as single completed actions and so they must be counted as genuine past tenses.

Many of the Cockney verbal parts, such as *growed* 'grew', *knowed* 'knew' and *throwed* 'threw', are formed by analogy – in these cases with forms like *mowed* and *sowed*. Since Anglo-Saxon times many originally strong verbs (which are those whose vowels changed in the past tense and past participle) became weak by simply adding *-ed* to the present stem, as *climb – climbed*[37]. Cockney, however, makes some weak past tenses and past participles foreign to Standard English, such as 'Them boys drahnded (drowned) yer moggy (cat)'; 'I've builded (built) a noo fence'.

The final *-n* of past participles of strong verbs, like most of those in the following list, often disappears. As late as 1794 it was still

accepted usage, but by Victorian times it was a vulgarism shown
e.g. in the writings of Dickens. In *Pickwick Papers*[38] Sam Weller says
'It's wrote', 'She was took ill' and 'I've eat four crumpets'.

Verb	*Past tense (preterite)*	*Past participle*
break	broke, *breaked*	*broke*
come	*come* (e.g. 'Yesterday, when I come back')	come
do	*done* ('E done 'is best)	done
drive	drove	*drove* (They was drove to it)
eat	*eat, ett*	eat(en), *ett* (I've only ett a sandwich)
forget	forgot	*forgot* (Yer've forgot again)
get	got, rarely *geet* (when we geet to the top)	got
give	*give* (A bloke give it me last night)	*give* ('E's give it 'er)
know	*noo, knowed, known*	*noo, knowed, known*
run	*run* (She run right under that car)	run
see	*seen, seed* (I seed it last week)	seen, *seed*
speak	spoke	*spoke* (It's most spoke of)
start	*Start* (Yest'dy afternoon when the Bow Bells start to ring)	*start*
steal	stole	*stole* (Mi bike's bin stole)
run	*run* ('E run right off)	run
take	took	*took* (They've took six)
write	wrote	*writ, wrote* (I 'adn't even wrote it)

Very typical of Cockney is the use of a past participle as a past
tense. It sounds as if a *has* or *have* has been forgotten, e.g. "E done
(did) noffink', 'We 'ad a feller what seen (who saw) it'. 'Do as that
lady done', I noticed a very Cockney street-seller urging after one
sale. He was trying to boost his pre-Christmas trade by sitting in a
shopping precinct on a very low stool, encircled by potential
customers and well out of sight of *coppers* who might spot him and
move him on. It is from such unusual parts of verbs that a detective

novel is popularly called a *whodunit* (from 'Who done, i.e. did, it?').
More educated Londoners become rather weary of this persistent
Cockney habit of mixing past tenses and past participles, but it is
well rooted in the dialect.

Favourite verbs for story-telling

In relating anecdotes the verb *to say* is repeated again and again,
especially by Cockney women, e.g. "E says to me, 'e says, "Did
yer?" an' I says "Course (of course) I did" an' then 'e says "Well,
that's a rum do (strange affair)" . . .'. Often we find, as in the last
set of remarks, the present historic tense, i.e. the present tense used
for past events. Here is a further example: 'I sees (saw) this feller, so
I goes (went) up to 'im an' I tells (told) 'im, an' 'e turns (turned)
rahnd an' says (said) . . .'.

Auxiliary verbs. Another type of repetition is of auxiliary along
with personal pronoun, e.g. "E didn't 'alf thump 'er, 'e did' (He hit
her hard); 'Goes like wildfire, that does' (That goes very fast);
'Took (mistook) me for a porter, he did'.

Can replaces *may* when asking permission, a widespread and
growing use throughout England, e.g. 'Can I come wiv yer?'

Outstanding is the shortening of auxiliary verbs both before a
main verb, as 'Ain't (Isn't) it goin'?', and enclitically, tagged onto
the ends of sentences, as 'Warm today, ain't it?' People grumble
about this widespread Cockney liking for *ain't*, but the thinking
Cockney replies that he has to keep saying it, especially for asking
questions, because it is so 'darned useful'.

This *ain't* is from *am not*, which became *ant* and *aint* and then
spread to other persons of singular and plural, as in Dickens[39]
where e.g. we find 'I ain't mistaken, ain't us?' 'an't this capital
(excellent)?'

Instead of *ain't it?* you may find *innit?* or *ennit?*. There are other
shortenings of auxiliary verbs, such as another *ain't* but this time by
loss of *v* for 'haven't' as in 'You ain't been there'. *Wonn it?* 'wasn't
it?', *Wun it?* 'wouldn't it?' and *Don' it?* 'Don't, i.e. doesn't it?' are
also commonly heard. Such shortenings have a long history, *warn't*
and *worn't* for 'wasn't' being used, for example, by Sam Weller in
Dickens. Various other auxiliary verbs have unusual tense forms,
in particular *mustn't* plus occasional *mawnt*, *daresn't* 'dare not', and
the long-sounding future type 'I ain't a-goin' to (shall not) do it'.

The oddest thing about Cockney tag-questions is their use to ask a listener things he or she cannot possibly know, especially in recounting incidents as: 'I'm goin' up the road, don' I? (was I not?)'; 'I'm goin' into 'im, don' I? (was fighting him, was I not?)'; 'I've gawn ter see 'im, don' I? (didn't I?)'; 'She fought (thought) she'd 'ave a joke wiv 'er mum, dint she? (did she not?)'. They correspond to strings of *you sees* and *you knows*, and act rather like grabbing a listener by the coat lapels to force him to hear the story.

Miscellaneous

Firstly, Cockney has no subjunctive, to use, for example, after *if* about things which could not happen. It is rare in Standard English, but Cockney manages quite happily without it altogether; e.g. in 'If I was you, I'd 'op it (run away)'. Standard English has here 'If I were you . . .' because *I* cannot be another person; but Cockney disdains such logic. Will Standard English itself soon follow suit? Secondly, strong stress can play havoc with choice of verb ('There 'ad use to be ware' ahses', i.e. there used to be) or verb ending ('Course it do' for '– it does'). Thirdly, Cockneys like many Standard English speakers are starting to use verbal forms in *-ing* for habits. They say e.g. 'John is workin' for the Post Orfice' when he is actually at the pub playing darts. In short, Cockney verbs take some deciphering.

Adjectives

Double comparatives occasionally occur, as *more safer* and *more uglier*. This happens in most English dialects. A not unduly modest Cockney helper declared of his mates, 'I noo (knew) I was much more cleverer than them', but he certainly was. Sometimes an almost redundant second adjective of very similar meaning is used for stress, e.g. *a li(tt)le tiny bi(t)* or *a great big 'un*.

Historically the articles *the* and *a* are special types of adjectives and so may be considered here. *The* appears, contrary to Standard English usage, with names of some illnesses as 'I've got the rheumatics', ''E's got the shakes (tremors)'; and *a* with days of the week, as 'I go rahnd the market on a Sa'urday mornin''.

Adverbs

Many adverbs end like their corresponding adjectives, without *-ly*. A Cockney will say: 'This car's runnin' slow (slowly)'; 'We can talk proper in London'; 'Yer've come in very quiet (quietly)'; 'I can't walk quick'.

Adverbial expressions show other irregularities, one being *as ah* for 'how', e.g. 'I don' know *as ah* yer does it'. This usage has existed in London dialect for over 200 years, since it is recorded in Bickerstaffe's farce *The Hypocrite*, written in 1769. 'Yes' is *yes*, or especially from youngsters *yeah* like American English, or very occasionally *ah* as in the S.W. Midlands. *Like* is frequently added to qualify expressions, as in 'I sort o' puts up wiv it, like (I endure it)'. *What for* equals 'Why', e.g. 'What did yer do it for?'; 'She kept shahtin' at me, I dunno what for'. *Pretty* is a common adverb of degree, as in 'I'm pretty (fairly) sure'. *That* works hard too as an adverb of degree, e.g. 'They was that mad (so angry)'; "'E's that pig-'eaded (so obstinate)'; 'She was that fru(tt)y', i.e. so untidy; 'She's that stuck-up (so snobbish)'; 'It's not that clever'. As for *that way on*, if you are so guided you will know to go 'in that direction'.

When story-telling, the Cockney has two irritating habits. One of them – and here the ladies are equal offenders with their menfolk – is to keep repeating *so*: 'So I goes to the laundrette an' so I gets the washin' done. Then mi ol' man (husband) comes back from work, so I gets 'is dinner, so 'e gollops it dahn (eats it greedily) . . .'. The other is *'cos why?*, which the Cockney answers immediately in an effort to air knowledge: 'I fixed a noo plug. 'Cos why? 'Cos the old 'un was bust'.

The Cockney system of multiplying negatives is nothing new. It was used by Chaucer, Ascham, Shakespeare and Pope. Chaucer, who lived in London, in his *Prologue to the Canterbury Tales* thus describes the Knight:

> *He never yet no villainie ne'er said*
> *In al his life, unto no maner wight (no kind of person).*

Using two *nos* is not like negative times negative in mathematics, making a positive 'yes': it just spreads the negative colouring over the whole sentence to make it still more negative. Though it is no Standard English, as has been expertly affirmed[40] 'you can' hardly beat a double negative for emphasis'. Examples from modern Cockney: 'She didn't take no notice'; 'They never 'ave noffink'; 'I ain't got none'; 'I never done it nohow (never did it at all)'. Even a string of three negatives is not too remarkable, e.g. 'We would*n't* *n*ever let 'im, *not* on yer life'.

Intensifiers

The Cockney has several intensifying adjectives and adverbs for 'very', e.g. 'I'm ree-u (*real*, very) pleased to see yer'; 'It's a tidy good (very long) way to walk to 'Arrer (Harrow)'; ''E's a reg'lar (very) good cobbler'; ''E's a right layabaht (great idler)'; 'She's a right ol' nosey-parker (very inquisitive person)'. Of these easily the commonest is *right*.

Cockney swear-adjectives, though very limited in range, are used so much, especially by workmen and less educated teenage youths, that they heavily colour the language. In the speech of some men, every second or third word seems to be a swear or sexual adjective. In fact, however, they have been so much over-used that they have lost practically all their meaning. They show a poverty of language and the shame is that this habit of being unable or unwilling to choose an appropriate intensifier has spread to younger people. In open-plan offices and among women (who think perhaps that it might harm their children's careers) and among the better educated it is much less common: but what was once thought ignorant or disgusting is now more or less accepted. George Bernard Shaw in his play *Pygmalion* shocked London audiences of 1930 when his flower-girl suddenly said in polite company 'Not bloody likely!' It would not shock audiences of, say, the Shaw Theatre off London's Euston Road today.

Intensifiers of this type range from *blinkin'*, *bloomin'* and *darned* where a stronger word like *bloody* or *damned* is twisted for politeness); through *bleedin'* and *bloody*, which is still the commonest swear-adjective (e.g. 'I've to go bloody nawf (north)'; to those with apparent sexual connotations like *soddin'* which have only recently been allowed into dictionaries. The last type, however, has lost practically all sexual significance, and such words are even used by children ignorantly trying to strengthen what they are saying. Intensifying adverbs are also created by adding *-well*, as: 'It's blinkin'-well bust (quite burst)', 'Yer bloody-well will (You certainly will)'.

Conjunctions

The conjunction which alters most is 'than', which is often shortened to *an* and occasionally becomes *nor*. Examples: 'owder an (older than) me'; 'dearer an (than) what they were'; 'worse nor (than) that'.

Yet, if we believe a well-known tale, the East End conjunctions, often equalling those of Standard English, cause more trouble to provincials. The story runs that a Yorkshireman and a *Geordie* visiting Cheapside saw a lights-controlled crossing for the first time. It bore the command, 'Do not cross while the light is red'. As everybody in those untamed parts of England knows, *while* means 'until'; and so they waited until it turned red. It was hard luck for the visitors, but they ended in the mortuary just the same.

Prepositions

These, as their name shows, are words like *from*, *on* and *to* which generally show position. In Cockney they are quite interesting. Consider:

1 Most characteristic of Cockney and the South-East, but beginning to spread to other parts of England, is *awf of* meaning just 'off'. The lengthened expression may seem unnecessary, but is used as a strengthening just as it was in Dickens. Present-day instances are: 'I seed (saw) 'er take it awf of the cahnter'; 'Get awf of the bus'. Another extra *of* is regular in cases like 'What yer (What do you) think yer doin' of?'

2 A reduction to *a* of the old preposition *on* before verbal nouns is sometimes heard, e.g. 'It's a-freezin'' from older *on-freezing*. Other examples are 'I'm a-usin' it; 'They've bin a-poachin''.

3 Then we have *of* confused with *on* because both can be reduced to *o'*, e.g. 'of a (on) Sunday'; 'there was only two on (of) us'; 'ge owd on (hold of) it'. Rather similar is 'took 'em awf of a (off at night'.

4 Sometimes *o'* standing for 'of' replaces 'with': 'It poured o (with) rain'; 'drownded o' water', though its last two words are hardly needed.

5 The insertion at other times of a quite unwanted *on*, e.g. 'usir on't (using it)'; 'suckin' on't (sucking it)'.

6 Miscellaneous: 'froo de wa' (through the wall)'; 'I've to se they're abed (in bed)'; 'just on eight year (about eight years)'.

Exclamations

Many of the rougher exclamations have been dealt with on page 51–54. Obviously there is a good deal of variety, from the *Ah!* as Cockney's eyes sparkle in anticipation of a good *nosh-up* to an *Oi!* he needs to attract attention and to the gasps of *Oo!* from his *kids* they unwrap their Christmas presents. Every Cockney has his favourites to add to traditional ones like *Gawd*!, *Love a duck*! and *Cor (God)! Stone the crows*! 'Good gracious!'

To sum up, then, many a Cockney may not know what grammar is; but, as the examples prove, unless he is *as dumb as a ditch*, he cannot do without it.

7
Pronunciation

Famous experts on the English language have differed on how to classify the traditional speech of London. In 1889 A.J. Ellis[41] divided England into 32 dialect areas. London falls into no less than four of these – no.8 which includes Surrey; no.9, including Kent; no.16, which includes most of Essex and Herts.; and no.17, which contains all older London north of the Thames.

Ellis states[42] 'I was myself born and passed my early life in the north of London'. Yet he adds a number of surprising statements, particularly the following about London north of the Thames: 'It is essentially a place where dialect could not grow up, because of the large mass of changing and more or less educated population'. Of London south of the river he made a similar judgment, asserting[43] that there 'dialect proper has been almost banished by town influence'.

Ellis could find no way of illustrating London speech through the 26 letters of the alphabet and invented his own phonetic script, which is extremely difficult even for phoneticians to interpret. He declares of North London [44], 'It would be impossible to illustrate this mode of speech by any approximate writing'. However, we are trying to do better by giving plenty of examples in approximate spelling with all its difficulties, supported in Appendix B, page 171, by phonetic symbols and charts based on the conventions of the International Phonetic Association.

Ellis also states that, especially since 1840, Essex forms took a greater and greater hold of London dialect and that perhaps by 1989 they would give it its general tone. Yet it would be highly abnormal for a surrounding county dialect to change a city dialect rather than the reverse, and we are now so near to 1989 that his prediction seems about to prove quite wrong. The answers about Cockney lie elsewhere.

Still introducing Cockney pronunciation, let us put two or three of its important sounds into historical perspective. The types of vowels which make 'boat race' sound almost like *bowt rice* are comparatively modern, occuring from about 1840. This may seem very long judged by our life span, but is little compared with the 1300 or so years of the English language. They were unknown to the compiler of the 1817 *Errors of Pronunciation* . . . and do not appear in *Pickwick Papers*, where they would have made ideal fun, or in the early volumes of *Punch*.

Words like 'now' and 'town' at present yield three types of vowels, which in historical order appear to be *nah* and *tahn*; *neh* and *tehn*; and most recently something like *ne-u* and *te-un*, which is nearest to Standard English.

All the leading Cockney sounds are summarised by Martyn Wakelin[45], who notes: 'The influence of popular London dialect with its characteristic sounds: roughly *a* tending towards *e* (*cab*); *o* in *off, cough* etc. tending towards *aw*; *uh* (*butter*) towards *a;* *ay* (*gate*) towards long *i* (RSE *fine* etc.); long *i* (*line, type*) towards *oi*; the sound in *no* towards that in *now*; *th* in *this, that* etc. becoming *d*; frequent use of the glottal stop (*bu'er, wa'er*); *l* becoming 'vocalised' to *oo* in *bull, field* (roughly *boo, fiood*). Many of these are also characteristic of Cockney proper, from which, however, we may add *ow* becoming an *ah* type of sound (*tahn, 'ahs*), *f* for *th* in *think*, and perhaps *aw* for *ah* in *heart, last*, etc.' I am glad that *perhaps* was cautiously inserted about the possible *aw* to *ah* change, for I have not heard it, but the summary is very good. After its help, we now take the Cockney sounds in turn, to see how far there still is a Cockney sound system and if so what patterns it makes.

A The vowels

Vowels are speech-sounds that could continue as long as you had enough breath. English has far more than the five vowels 'a, e, i, o and u' learnt through school spelling. Amongst other things, they are greatly affected by where the tongue-top is in the mouth. For a vowel in any language or dialect in the world, the tongue-top can move only in the shaded area shown in the drawing overleaf. Clearly, to repeat a diagram like this every time we wanted to explain a vowel would be utterly time-wasting, and so it is usual to show just an enlargement of the shaded area. Such a system is used here to illustrate some of the Cockney vowels. Where the tongue-tip moves during the vowel, the arrow shows the direction of the movement. For scientific accuracy, the vowels appear also in phonetics in Appendix B. The dotted lines are just guide-lines.

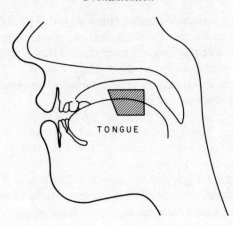

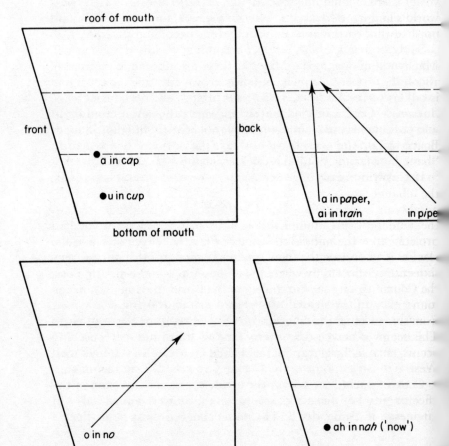

roof of mouth

front

back

● a in c*a*p

● u in c*u*p

a in p*a*per,
ai in tr*ai*n

in p*i*pe

bottom of mouth

o in n*o*

● ah in n*ah* ('now')

Note. Vowels of any language or dialect have to be sufficiently distinct not to be confused. For example, if in Cockney 'paper' begins to sound like *piper*, then 'piper' will have to be pronounced rather like *poiper*. Similarly, if the Cockney vowel in 'no' sounds rather like that in *now*, then its 'now' changes, most traditionally to *nah*. One move causes another.

Now we examine words according to the vowels they had in Middle English, which helps to determine what vowels they have today.

Short stressed vowels

ME (MIDDLE ENGLISH) *a* (E.G. IN *man*, *bag*) In Cockney ME *a* is raised to a sound midway between *a* and *e*, and often to *e* itself. The vowel is fairly long. The midway sound is an unusual one in the world's languages, and has been compared, though Cockneys will not like this, to the noise of a sheep bleating.

Such a raised sound has long been characteristic of the dialect. Machyn in his 1550–63 diary spelt *messe* 'mass' and *then* 'than'. In 1890 Ellis[46] stated, 'There is a peculiar thinness about *a* . . . which is odious to people from other parts of England'. The *Kaukneigh Awlmineck* 'Cockney Almanac' of 1883 had *bed men* for 'bad man', and the previous year the Rev. D'Orsey had written to the School Board of London that 'the use of *keb, benk, strend* (i.e. for "cab", "bank", "Strand") . . . may be growing'.

H.C. Wyld[47] has a lucid account of its development, stating that the change towards *e* 'began in the South-Eastern counties, notably in Essex in the fifteenth century. . . . Only gradually did the tendency spread to London, and at first only among the proletariat or the middle classes. . . . From the lower and middle classes in London the new pronunciation passed during the sixteenth century to the upper classes, and even into the English of the Court. Among the latter sections of the community the fronted sound may quite possibly have been at first an affectation adopted from some feeling that it was more refined than the "broader" *a*'. This seems a good explanation because today the raised sound occurs only in East Anglia, the Home Counties and the South-West.

Cockneys may be the butt of sly digs about their apparently affected *e* for *a*, but they in turn can joke at the Northerner's attempts to deal with the sound. For example, they know instinctively that *Pall Mall* is pronounced almost like *Pell Mell* (as Pepys spelt it); and I have heard them burst into uncontrollable laughter at a Northerner's *Pawl Mawl* when the Northerner could not see what was causing the merriment.

Before the sounds *s*, *f*, or *n* followed by another consonant, Cockney like Standard English has the 'long a'. Thus it sounds, e.g., as if he walks up the *pahf* (path) to visit his *ahnt* (aunt), or has to stop his daughter having a *lahst dahnce* on the *grahs* near Windsor *Cahstle*. Those who use the 'short a' in such words think that 'long a' speakers sound affected, whilst the Cockney thinks that 'short a' is provincial. We all make *ah*-sounds, as when the doctor asks to examine our tongues, and it is just a matter of agreeing which words should have them. The Cockney is in no doubt.

ME *o* (E.G. IN *not*, *off*)   Before *f* or *s*, as in older-fashioned English and the speech of the Queen, this is still an *aw*-sound. Thus *sawft soap, acrawss the lawft, it's gawn awf*; also *dish-clawf* 'dish-cloth'. This sound in such words is of great antiquity – compare *ffauster lane* 'Foster Lane'[48], written in 1487.

ME *u* (E.G. IN *put*, *cup*)   From Middle English short *u* we get the rounded sound *uh* appearing in words like *could, should* and *would*; and in other words chiefly next to a lip-rounded consonant, e.g. in *wood, wool; bull, bullet; push, put; book, look, shook*. This tallies with Standard English. However, in a greater number of terms spelt mostly with *u*, such as *but, butter, mud, nut, shut, rough, tough, flood* and *bloody* (i.e. very) *funny*, Cockney uses a type of *u* verging on *a*, so that 'mud and blood' resembles *mad 'n' blad*; and you seem invited to have a *cap*, not *cup*, of tea. This creation of two vowels for only one in Middle English may well have its origin in social dialect[49]. Why else, for example, do Cockneys say a rounded *uh* in *put* but use their *u* which is nearly *a* in *putt*? Golf used to be a game of the wealthy

Long vowels and diphthongs (combinations of two vowels)
ee AND *oo* (AS IN *eat, seat, tree; cool, soon, tooth*)   Neither 'long ee (from ME *ē*) nor 'long oo' (from ME *ō₁*) is a pure vowel in Cockney, for during each of them the tongue-tip moves. George Bernard Shaw was the first to point this out, in his description of the alphabet he heard being recited as he passed a Cockney elementary school:

Letter	Shaw's spelling of what he heard
A	I
B	Ber-ee
C	Ser-ee
D	Der-ee
E	Er-ee
F	Aff
G	Jer-ee
H	Iche
I	Awy
J	Ji
K	Ki
L	Al
M	Am
N	An
O	Ow
P	Per-ee
Q	Kioo
R	Aw
S	Ass
T	Ter-ee
U	Yer-eoo
V	Ver-ee
W	Dabble-yew
X	Ax
Y	Wawy
Z	Zad

His use of *a* in *Aff, Al, Am, An, Ass, Ax* and *Zad* for the Standard English sound *e* is somewhat unusual. Certainly I have not noticed it in modern Cockney. In addition, the following notes on separate long vowels and diphthongs suggest that he may have exaggerated other matters not readily discernible in current speech.

ME *ā* AND *ai* (E.G. IN *same, tail*)   For both these sounds the Standard English equivalent is *ay*, whereas Cockney uses a diphthong with much more tongue movement approaching an *I*. In 1882 the Rev. A.J.D. D'Orsey, who was professor of the public speaking at King's College, wrote to the School Board for London that in the city 'Such words as *paper, shape, train* are pronounced *piper, shipe, trine*'. Ellis, writing eight years later[50], states that D'Orsey meant a vowel not quite reaching *I* and that this vowel was strongest in East and North London, 'being as yet comparatively little developed in North-West and West London'. He continues, 'But it is recent . . . I was myself born in N. London in 1814 and cannot recall it', adding that pronunciations like *piper* for paper were unknown in London before about 1840. Yet old spellings like *obtyning* 'obtaining' (1589) and *Rile* 'royal' (1623), both from Machyn, suggest that it was used, at least by some Cockneys, much earlier. The important thing now is that, regardless of exactly when it started, the vowel has spread throughout London and indeed to great stretches of the East and Central Midlands, including Birmingham.

A more educated but still a Cockney variant, and quite common, is *ey* with less tongue movement than in broad Cockney but more than in Standard English. Thus 'What did the leydy sey?'. It came into use in Essex by the younger generation in the 1880s[51].

ME ī (E.G. IN *light, time, sky*)   This sound had changed right back in the seventeenth century, for early London documents include spellings[52] such as *ploying* 'playing' in 1614 and *hoye* 'high' in 1633. However, these spellings are a trifle deceptive. In 1882 D'Orsey wrote that in Cockney '*light* is almost *loyt*', and Ellis agreed that it reached *ah-i* but that he himself had not observed an actual *oi*. Very occasionally I hear a full *oi*, but easily the commonest today also is *ah-i*.

ME $\bar{o}_2$ (IN *boat* ETC.)   Words like *boat, home, loaf*, and *coat, hole, throat* have a sound approaching an *ow*, so that 'Oh, we've no coats' resembles 'Ow, we've now cowts'. This is another Cockney sound of which the uninformed Northerner tries to make great fun.

ME ū (E.G. IN *house*)   This as explained has three basic develop-ments. First is a glideless *aht-and-abaht* type, older and better-known in writing because it is easier to represent by letters of the alphabet, e.g. *Lunnon Tahn, rahnd an' rahnd de 'ahses*. It is also the one most often mocked (*Ah nah, brahn cah!*). Marketmen still use this pronunciation, which Matthews[53], by talking to very old Cock-neys from around Hoxton about their boyhood experiences proved must have been spoken from at least 1865. Later came an *eh-er* type and still later *e-u*. All three types are widely heard, but their social ranks depend upon their nearness to the Standard English equivalent *ow*. Lowest therefore in social status is *ah*, highe is *eh-er* because at least it is a diphthong (two vowels), highest is *e-*

because not only is it a diphthong but it finishes very like Standard English *ow*. But even *e-u* has come in for its share of criticism. Wyld objected to middle-class Cockneys using it and calls it, though only humorously, 'a typical mark of the beast', i.e. an animal-like sound[54]. As Ellis noted in the nineteenth century[55], there is a tendency towards *e-u* even among many well-educated Londoners.

ME ȳ (IN *duke* ETC.)   In Standard English this gives *yoo* but in Cockney just *oo*, as: *a noo soot* (new suit), *the dook* (duke), *What's the toon* (tune)?

ME *oi* (E.G. IN *oil*, *point*)   In the writings of Charles Dickens, this is represented by an *i* standing for the *I*-type of sound which formerly occurred in such words in Standard English (The *oi* in our *oil*, *poison*, etc. is a spelling pronunciation). In *Pickwick Papers*, London's Sam Weller pronounces 'boil' as *bile*. Similarly Mayhew, when he represents Cockney speech, often spells words of the *toil* type with *i*. Thus with him 'boil' becomes *b'ile* or *bile*, 'joint' becomes *jint*, etc., suggesting that *point* may have rhymed with *pint*, and *toy* with *tie*, etc., in the London vernacular of the 1860s. But today the feature seems to have died out.

Unstressed vowels

FINAL -*er* (E.G. IN *player*, *China*)   A striking Cockney feature, though rarely commented upon, is the way this vowel resembles a short *ah*. It makes what is in Standard English a 'blurred' central vowel sound unusually precise, as if the Cockney is continually making important announcements. For example, 'I'm de drivah (the driver)' sounds as if he is without question a tip-top motorist, and "Ang up de pictyah' as if he expects his house walls to be adorned with a Rembrandt. To Englishmen from other parts of the country it sounds rather comical, since English unlike some other languages (e.g. many African ones) has no short *ah* at the ends of words. This Cockney vowel occurs also to end various diphthongs, giving results like 'I don't ce-ah for the paw-ah bee-ah (care for the poor beer)'.

It has, however, won a pale glimmer of fame as a brand of what is called *Cockney rhyme*[56], which is an imperfect rhyme in Standard English which rhymes when given a popular London accent. Rupert Brook, who teased others with making such errors, fell into one himself:

But laughing and half-way up to heaven,
With wind and hill and *star*,
I yet shall keep, before I sleep,
Your Ambervali*a*.

Other unstressed vowels

In unstressed positions there is a preference for *i*, more so than in
Standard English and far more than in the northern counties.
Cockney has *i*, for example, in *Billingsgit* 'Billingsgate', *Cripplegit*
'Cripplegate', *gardin* 'garden' and *'addick* 'haddock'. Unstressed
-ow is weakened. That is why Cockney markets teem with *barrers*
and *barrer-boys*, and on nearby buildings *sparrers* flit about the *narrer*
winders. Extra unstressed vowels sporadically burst forth, as at the
fillams 'films' when one of the fair sex gasps 'Ain't it luvverly
(lovely)!'

B Consonants

We shall take only those consonants which differ in use and/or
sound from those of Standard English, treating them as far as
possible in alphabetical order.

INITIAL *h-* This usually disappears, as in most English dialects,
e.g. *'It 'im 'ard! Fetch a 'eavy 'ammer*. Destitute Stepney families used
to be thrilled at the Christmas gift of *anampah* 'a hamper' from the
fund of a benevolent ex-Lord Mayor. Unfortunately, when
Cockneys take great pains to be careful, they are very prone to
wrongly inserting *h*s. E.g. 'Hi ham 'ere to hopen this hexcellent
'all'. Such confusion, which can be quite embarrassing, arises from a
vague knowledge that spelling has more *h*s than are usually said.

l Cockneys use a 'dark l', i.e. one formed by raising the middle
and back of the tongue. George Bernard Shaw was the first
important writer to recognise this, for he uses spellings like *'eolth*
'health', *teoll* 'tell' and *weoll* 'well'. In fact the *l* is often so 'dark' that
it ceases to be an *l* at all and turns into the vowel *u*, as in 'We-u, we
aw-u fe-u on de baw-u as it row-ud dahn de i-u (Well, we all fell on
the ball as it rolled down the hill)'. In 1952, when considering the
speech of South Hackney schoolchildren, I found that their final *l*s
often disappeared into the vowel *u*; and that throughout the
London area the *l* was so 'dark' that it very often produced answers
like *schoo-u* 'school' and *frai-u* 'frail'. Today the situation is no
different.

FINAL -*ng* IN 'TAKING', ETC. Two things can happen here. Cockneys often 'drop the g', as it is generally termed, so that 'taking' becomes *takin'*, 'shopping' becomes *shoppin'* etc., although really no g-sound is involved, for the nasal sound *ng* is represented by another nasal one, *n*. This sound-change is quite old – compare the aristocratic practice of *huntin'*, *shootin'* *and fishin'*. But many Cockneys, especially for 'something', 'nothing' and 'anything', finish with a -*k*, saying *somefink, noffink, anyfink*. This second type also has a long history, for in 1787 Elphinston stated 'a common Londoner talks of *anny think else*, or *anny thing kelse'*. That solves the mystery of 'dropping the g'.

r London's *r* is normally the fricative *r* of Standard English. Some East Enders, including some of the more educated, pronounce instead a *w*, saying e.g. that the weather is *fwawsty* 'frosty' or that they would like a *dwink*. Although it seems chiefly an individual matter, Greater London does appear to have a larger percentage of *w*-for-*r* people than do other parts of the country. It may be relevant to point out here that a surprising number of well-known politicians and 'captains of industry' bred in the South-East have had this outstanding *w*.

London does not have the retroflex, deeply throated *r* of the South and South-West of England except very occasionally on its southern fringe and some of its east central districts.

As in Standard English, London's *r* disappears in saying words like *far, four, hard, beard*. The extinction by the metropolis of such an *r* is very ancient. According to H.C. Wyld,[57] by 1550 London speakers of the humbler sort besides better educated ones hardly pronounced such an *r*. In his 1785 *Rhetorical Grammar*, John Walker stated that it had disappeared 'particularly in London' in *bar, bard, card*, etc., which were pronounced as *baa*, etc. Opposite to this *r* which is spelt but not pronounced, is the Cockney 'intrusive r' which is sounded though absent from the spelling. It is a linking *r*, to help the tongue to move smoothly from one vowel to the next. After an unstressed -*er* sound, as in 'I'd better open it', this 'ghost r' passes almost unnoticed because in such positions it is allowed also in Standard English. Here we are far more tolerant than the 1817 London speech pamphlet which poured scorn on *Idear, for Idea*[58].

After other vowels, especially *aw*, an 'intrusive *r*' annoys many people, particularly provincials, because it sounds quite foreign to them and neither is it Standard English. Cockneys who use it in this unorthodox fashion talk, for example, of *saw-r-in'* wood, the *draw-r-in'-office* 'drawing-office', and *jaw-r-in'* 'jawing', i.e. gossiping. They say *Pa-r-an' Ma-r-are aht* 'Pa and Ma are out'; and when the snow melts, for it never stays long in London, *It's thaw-r-in'*.

Glottal stops

The most striking consonantal feature of the dialect is what is often known as 'missing the *t*s', though in fact many *k*s and *p*s also disappear. In their places are put glottal stops, which are complete breaks in the stream of sound rather like gentle coughs. They are used by Cockneys abundantly for *t*, quite often for *k*, and by broad-spoken Cockneys even for *p*.

The glottal stop is a prominent feature of British city dialects, where it is still spreading though not yet characteristic of a few cities in Northern England such as Liverpool and Carlisle. London is the city in which it is most deeply entrenched.

It is generally thought to be a quite recent development, but was in fact used in earlier Cockney. In 1882 Professor D'Orsey noted how hard it was to differentiate *like* and *light* in Cockney pronunciation, presumably because both were heard as *li'*; and Richard Whiteing's 1899 spelling *Hy' Par'* for Hyde Park confirms that glottal stops were established in the city by the end of last century. In 1915 it was amusingly explained by Alfred Anscombe[59]: 'Ivver 'ear tell er the "glottal stop"? Yew dinow waut the glo'al staup es? Well, HI'll tell yer. 'Few truy (If you try) ter saigh "lucky" wivaout the ck you'll git eet: lu'y, see? They've gaut eet in Glasgow an' we've gaut eet in London. . . . F'rinstance, we saigh mu'on an bu'on. . . .'

Young Cockneys use even more of these glottal stops than their elders, so the feature shows no sign of dying out. They occur most often between vowels, or between vowel and *l*, *r* for *e* or *w*; but they can appear in other contexts, e.g. quite often finally in a word. Examples: *Gi' u' 'ere* 'Get up here', *Cla'am Cawmmon* 'Clapham Common', *Tha' blo' wants some bra'ets* 'That bloke wants some brackets', *a li'le bi' quie'er* 'a little quieter', 'There's fru'ence (threepence) in the gu'er (gutter)'. *'Ay'ah!* (Paper!) shouts the Cockney newsboy, inserting two glottal stops in one word.

Variations in the glottal stop occur. Sometimes *k*s, *p*s and *t*s are half strangled by glottal stops and only weakly exploded. And London teachers, especially the ladies, can become so incensed at a constant barrage of glottal stops that they go to the opposite extreme of over-stressing the *t*, e.g. 'Please, miss, 'e's pu' i' in 'is 'a' (put it in his hat)', drawing the angry query 'In his whaT?'.

th Another well-known Cockney feature is to replace the voiceless and voiced sounds spelt *th*, which started according to H.C. Wyld[60] in the fifteenth and sixteenth centuries with spellings like *Frogmorton* 'Throgmorton' and *bequived* 'bequeathed'. Wyld called it 'a very low type of Cockney English', although whether all Cockneys now using it would agree is another matter.

Unvoiced *th* becomes *f* and parallel to it voiced *th* becomes *v*. Examples: *fanks* 'thanks', *bof fings* 'both things', *it's worf noffink* (worth nothing), *I fought* (thought) *we 'ad free* (three); *don't bovver wiv me ovver brovver* 'don't bother with my other brother'.

This simplification of voiced and unvoiced *th* is not so surprising since they are rare sounds in the world's languages. Indeed quite a number of English children from all parts of the country have trouble with them, and unless their faults are corrected early go on saying e.g. *teef* 'teeth' and *movver* 'mother' for some years. It is most doubtful whether this supports any claim that Cockney speech is more childish than that of other places (*childlike* in its sounds might possibly be a fairer description), but the substitutes for *th* do occur far more often in London than elsewhere.

Since at least the sixteenth century, another Cockney way of avoiding the voiced *th* has been to replace it by a *d* as in *Bednall Green* 'Bethnall Green' in Machyn's Diary. This is less common than it used to be, but still liable to crop up, especially in the very useful words *de* 'the', *dis, dat, dese, dose, den* and *deir*. Younger Cockneys often produce a mixture of *d* and *th* rather than a full *d*.

INTERCHANGE OF *v* AND *w* This interchange is well-known to readers of Dickens, Thackeray and the early numbers of *Punch*, which are liberally sprinkled with examples like *ven* 'when', *vy* 'why'; *werry* 'very', *wiolet* 'violet'. A *v* for *w* was apparently a genuine sound-substitution because recent earthquake-refugees to England from the island of Tristran da Cunha, whose ancestors came from S.E. England, have this *v*. There was indeed an old Cockney conundrum which exemplified this 'error'[61]. It ran, 'Why is a pocket-handkerchief like a species of serpent? Because it is a viper'. Professor Wyld[62] remembered people saying jocularly *vich* 'which' and *weal* 'veal', apparently imitating the speech of those they had heard in their childhood about 1850; but all commentators seem to agree that in London *v* for *w* died out shortly afterwards. The only people who use it in London today are some of the overseas immigrants.

The *w* for *v* lasted longer. Professor E. Weekley stated that in the 1870s he quite often heard old Cockneys of the humblest class using it. In 1890 Ellis recorded having obtained it in Essex, not far from London, in *wery* 'very', *wessels* 'vessels', *winegar* 'vinegar', *wittle* 'victual' and *woice* 'voice'. Matthews found that by the 1880s *w* for *v* was used by only a few old Cockneys and was generally considered comic. My London searches from the last war onwards have never revealed it in natural use. Therefore, despite old Mr Weller in Dickens who spelt his surname with 'a we', and despite other writings and music-hall songs, we must regard this quaint feature as extinct.

Nasalisation

This is quite noticeable in Cockney. It is a hated feature of many British city dialects (most notoriously in Liverpool speech and that of Birmingham). In Cockney it seems most marked in vowels followed by the nasal sounds *m* or *n*, as in '*ammer, a fine mornin*', or *rank* meaning 'reasty' (of butter or bacon). But over the whole speech, not just round Cockney's *m*s and *n*s, there usually lies a faint tinge of nasalisation.

All sorts of theories have been brought forward to try to explain it. It has been attributed, for example, to pollution in the city atmosphere from smog created by factory chimneys or from traffic fumes. However, if its chief cause is always pollution, there must have been pollution in France for a very long time. Some experts claim of the nasalisation in London and many other places (e.g. in America) that it began by sheer accident and was then imitated. Its chief causes in Cockney appear to be little movement of the lips and jaw, and the Cockney fondness for centralised vowels. At any rate, whatever the reason, nasalisation is another continuing characteristic of the dialect.

Speed of talk

Naturally, just how fast someone talks varies with the speaker, his or her mood (excited, sad, afraid, etc.) and the subject being discussed. Some women (and rather fewer men) resort to a drawling of accented syllables to give certain words stronger emphasis, e.g. *Imposs . . . ible!, Fasc . . . inating!*

However, the general tendency of Cockney speech is the opposite, to talk somewhat faster than the average Britisher. This makes it even more difficult for someone from overseas to understand, although of course, when they know that they are explaining to someone from abroad, e.g. in giving directions, Cockneys will out of politeness and sympathy talk extra slowly. Normal Cockney talk is fairly quick. This is in line with what tape-recordings show is usual in British cities. It may well be connected with the faster pace of life in the metropolis – things happen so rapidly in the hustle and bustle of London that you feel you must say what you want quickly before the chance goes.

This greater speed of talk is achieved in many ways. London's glottal stops, common especially amongst men, youths and children, give its speech a 'clipped' effect. Secondly, instead of being replaced by a glottal stop, an intervocalic -t- may become -r-, which trips easily from the tongue to give a rapid bullet-like effect, especially when normal word-divisions also break down, e.g.: *Yerlattergerrawf* 'You will have to get off'; *Lerrinfirrit* 'Let him fit it'; *Gerrahravit!* 'Get out of it!', i.e. 'Go away!'; *Itsgorralorravoles* 'It has got a lot of holes'. The same sense of urgency makes *t*s disappear from other places, as 'I wonna (want to) go nah!'

A further impetus to faster speech comes from losing an initial syllable when the main stress arose originally on the second, e.g. *cos* 'because', *lastic* 'elastic', *lastoplast* 'elastoplast', *lectric* 'electric(ity)', *prentice* 'apprentice', *tice* 'entice', *Scuse me* 'Excuse me'. Surprisingly, a stressed syllable is lost in *Kyoo* 'Thank you' – often said although rarely written like that. *Ain't it?* is another well-known shortening. Sometimes whole words disappear, as from *Gotcher!* '(I have) got you!' 'Streets what run side (which run at the side of, or beside) the Thames', 'E's aht the back (out at the back)'. For such reasons, London talk is comparatively fast.

Lest it be thought this analysis is heavily biased for or against rapid speech, some other opinions should be mentioned. Some outsiders say, 'Does it really matter if Londoners do talk faster, or if their good ladies do tend to gabble more. They gabble lucidly'. Others protest, 'Country folk, speaking in a drawl, may have a more sincere style of telling a story. Anyway, we hate Cockneys even more than *Brummagers* because they're too damned quick for us'. The reader must judge.

Loudness

In very general terms, Londoners seem to talk a little more loudly
than their provincial friends. This we may put down to having to
cope with the continual clamour of the bustling metropolis – if you
have to urge a *Billingsgit* porter to move fish-boxes from a lorry, you
do not confide in him in a gentle Cockney *whispah*. There are many
East Enders whose telephone voices suggest that they don't really
believe the lines work!

Jamaican women immigrants at opposite ends of a London bus
seem especially prone to talking to each other in shouts, which may
perhaps be excused as they come from an island with lots of space.
But this does not apply to, say, Poplar housewives bawling at each
other in a friendly way from neighbouring flats. To make a
scientific count of decibels would be hard and perhaps ultimately
of little use, but Cockney appears undisputed champion of the
loudness league-table.

Intonation

This is still a barely researched subject, but there is space to draw
attention to two points about it that spring immediately to mind.
Cockney males usually seem to have a somewhat 'flatter', monotonous intonation, greater pitch variations coming from the ladies.
Is this because the latter are more excitable? Secondly – not often
but apparently more so than in the provinces – there is sometimes a
continually dropping intonation in questions, as:

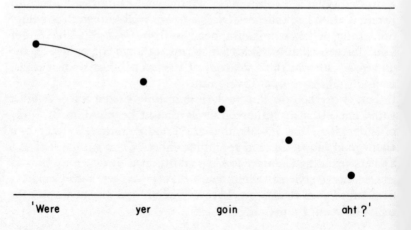

'Were   yer   goin   aht ?'

It sounds rather weary, for normally in Cockney as in other British dialects the pitch rises at question-ends. If this area of language could be minutely investigated, doubtless Cockney like, say, Scottish and Welsh forms of English, would be found to have its special intonation patterns.

General impressions

Just to show how greatly London's vowels and consonants have been affected, comparing A.W. Tuer's 1885 booklet *Old London Street Cries* it is interesting to see how strangely the names of stations have been announced on the Inner Circle tube railway. According to him – and it is little different today – only one name, that of *Gower Street*, is regularly pronounced as in Standard English, probably because it is the nearest stop to that enormous and splendid institution, London University. Others include: *Emma Smith, Emma Smif* 'Hammersmith'; *Sahf Kensin'n* 'South Kensington'; *Glawster Rowd* 'Gloucester Road' (where *Rowd* rhymes almost with BBC *loud*); *Nottin' 'Ill Gite* 'Notting Hill Gate'; *Edge-wer Rowd* 'Edgeware Road'; *Biker (Baker) Street; King's Krauss (Cross)*, often abbreviated to 'ngs Krauss; *Monneym'nt* 'Monument'; *Kennun (Cannon) Street; Menshun Aas* 'Mansion House'; *Wes'minster,* and occasionally *Wes'minister* with an extra *i* just like that which can slip into *Admirality Arch; S'n James-iz Pawk* 'St James's Park'; *Victaw-ia* 'Victoria'; *Peddin'n* 'Paddington'; *Bishergit* 'Bishopgate'; *Oldersgit (Aldersgate) Street.*

To the outsider, the phonetics of Cockney are quite baffling. Wherever you go in London, you may hear from time to time cries resembling *Light piper!* 'Late paper' and *Aw de lavverly noos!* 'All the lovely news', as well as the tubeman's warning *Mine ors!* for 'Mind (Beware) the doors!' or *Parsdon Karspeas* 'Pass down the cars, please!' These cries take some understanding and one wonders how Japanese and other overseas visitors to London, even if equipped with phrase books and helped by knowlegeable native guides, can make head or tail of them. Visitors from other parts of Britain would find it most instructive to listen hard to tube-station announcements, street-cries and most importantly free conversation of all kinds. Cockneys themselves are in little need of such help (though sceptics might argue that they are beyond help). In the last resort, they are the best experts on their *pronounciation.*

8
Sociology

Sociology has never been far from the matters we have been discussing, for Cockney dialect is one spoken in a particular society. Sometimes, as when we dealt with rhyming slang and coarse language, sociology has loomed quite large. As we have also seen, social class is too an important factor in pronunciation, e.g. in whether the Londoner says *name* as on the BBC, or something approaching *nime* like a true Cockney, or something in between like *neym*. But now we turn to matters that are primarily sociological, though of course they are also linked with language.

A great social gulf has long existed between London's West and East Ends, shown for instance in 1712 in Pope's satirical poem *Rape of the Lock*[63]. When Belinda has had her beautiful locks of hair shamefully cut off by the Baron, he writes that so impossible was it that she should want him to gaze on her that:

'Sooner shall grass in Hyde-park Circus grow,
And wits take lodgings in the sound of Bow'.

Many people – and not only *uppers* 'upper-class' from the West End – have violent objections to Cockney. They label it 'monotonous', 'ugly', 'horrible', 'harsh', and seem to equate it with the dreadful sameness of the housing projects and towering office blocks in London. It has also been called 'confused', 'whining', 'weak and flabby', etc. – hardly ever is it described in a kindly way.

Attacks of this kind are not new. In 1923 E. Gepp in compiling his *Essex Dialect Dictionary* grumbled[64] about the 'ugly vernacular sounds' of unliterary Londoners, and warns his readers 'Modern Cockney language has now crept in among us, and is creeping more and more, and we regret and resent it'. And again, 'the deadening influence of London is seen for many miles out . . . the poison is in the air, and the blighting Cockney's *Sahfend* (Southend), *Borking* (Barking) and *Elstead* (Halstead) and the like show us what we may come to. Heaven preserve us!'

This is surely a very biased attitude. Such judgments are based on instinct or snobbery, not scientific accuracy. Sounds are just sounds, words are meaningful collections of sounds, and grammar is the necessary way to link words in sentences. We should never call another dialect, or another language for that matter, 'uncouth', 'ugly', etc. just because we cannot immediately understand it.

It is a great mistake to brand all Cockneys as laughable and nothing else. Some outsiders actually believe that East Enders must be a bit *potty* to live in such a place, but they have little choice; and vast numbers of Cockneys, like people everywhere, are warm-hearted, friendly and would do anything for anybody. Human nature does not change – some people are greedy and others quite unselfish – and it cannot suddenly be altered by domiciling a Cockney on the fringes of *'Ampstead 'Eaf* or in miserable rooms near Gardener's Corner.

Cockney like other forms of language is a social medium, and Cockneys talk like people around them. To talk differently from their neighbours would set them off as strange. The *telly* and *wireless* may broadcast prestige English, but audiences do not talk back to them; and for a Cockney child five hours a day in school (only on average three if week-ends and holidays are counted) is very little compared with all the time spent with friends and family.

Cities have a mixture of regional dialect and Standard English, and this is especially so for London, where the language of the East End Cockney intermingles with that of the daily commuter and the stockbroker. London speech can be considered a pyramid, its horizontal plane representing the region and its vertical plane that of its various social dialects. London may have a business tycoon and a *dusty* born in the same small district but with very different language. The dustman will speak much dialect and slang and so be near the base of the pyramid, whereas the tycoon owing to the linguistic demands of his job will be near its apex.

With children as with adults, marked differences of dialect arise within central London. Islington schoolchildren, it is reported, talk of having *lots o' lolly* or being *quids in*, and say of a proud person *'e reckons 'imself*; uphill at Highgate, a better-class area although now very much hemmed in by developments towards the North Circular Road, children talk correspondingly of being *well-to-do*, having *plenty of money* and being *conceited*. These are differences of social dialects. Children's swearing is also largely determined by social factors. Answers of pupils from Tottenham School and from Kingsmead School, Hackney, on a 1977 BBC educational programme in the series *Speak* about 'bad language', showed that many did not go onto football-ground terraces where swearing was prevalent, chiefly because they came from a reasonably high social background and consequently felt that such swearing was ignorant and mindless.

People have had such extreme views about Cockney. The 1909 report of the Conference on the Teaching of English in London Elementary Schools was most scathing: 'The Cockney mode of speech, with its unpleasant twang, is a modern corruption without legitimate credentials, and is unworthy of being the speech of any person in the capital city of the Empire'. Here value judgments pour out. A more reasoned view was that of Edwin Pugh in *Harry the Cockney* (1902): 'The average Cockney is not articulate. He is often witty; he is sometimes eloquent; he has a notable gift of phrase-making and nick-naming. Every day he is enriching the English tongue with new forms of speech, new clichés, new slang, new catchwords. The new thing and the new word to describe the new thing are never far apart in London. But the spirit, the soul, of the Londoner, is usually dumb'. This assessment, despite some exaggeration towards its end, is a better one, showing Cockney's attractions along with its limitations.

Unnecessary hostility about their birthplaces flares up today amongst some better educated Londoners. A recent letter from a Clapham lady to the *Evening Standard*[65] seeks to 'undermine the snotty north Londoner's attitude to the Other Side of the River' with its 'mixed population that is more alive than the boring middle-class zombies of the snobbier side of the Thames', and declares 'It is time South Londoners stopped thinking they are inferior – we're not'. Although London is so vast that it must contain extremes of human wretchedness and luxury, such bickering between, say, the traditional deprived Cockney areas of Stepney and Bermondsey, even though they lie on opposite sides of the Thames, would be almost unheard of.

A fascinating question is how high Cockney stands in the 'pecking order' of British city dialects. Exhaustive questioning round the country indicates that it is far less universally despised than *Scouse* or *Brum*, names given respectively to Liverpool and Birmingham speech with their strongly nasal qualities; but that

Cockney is thought less attractive than, for example, Bristol or Exeter language with their quaint south-western tinges and possibly bringing memories of pleasant holidays in those sunny parts of England. It is generally rated slightly above half-way in the table of British city dialects, probably because it is thought dangerous and wrong to criticise too severely any speech layer in what is after all our prime city.

Another intriguing question is whether the dialect changes from area to area within London regardless of social conditions. George Bernard Shaw claimed through his character Professor Higgins in *Pygmalion* that all varieties of London dialect could be narrowed down to a location 'within two miles. Sometimes within two streets', but this claim was for theatrical purposes. People often boast that they can tell the speech of one district from that of another, but when pressed they become vague except for giving instances of social distinctions in words and sounds. Some think that the Surrey side of London talks differently from central and north London, and for this there is some slight evidence (occasional reverted 'Southern' *r* and occasional full *oi*-sound in words like *time* on the southern edge of London); but the general picture today is of a dialect changing socially through many layers but geographically hardly at all within the vast sprawl of the capital; e.g. some natives of Battersea claim they can recognise a *Ba'ersea grahl* (growl) from its deeper tone. This is arguable; but, even if it is occasionally correct, it remains true that what helps most to distinguish the speech of one Battersea native from that of his neighbour are his social aspirations.

Shop and stall language

Although London's Cockney dialect is strong, behind the counters of all shops and department stores it is thinned down simply in order to be polite and well understood by any customer. Even so, there can remain astonishing differences, although as the years roll by they are quickly weakening. It is well worth listening yourself to detect such differences. Much less Cockney dialect will be heard in a high-class store like Harrods' than in, say, an equally useful one like Woolworth's, where most people are perhaps from a working-class or lower working-class background.

Street stallholders' language is likely to be more robust. One I recorded was holding up bottles of perfume. His patter went:

'They'll say these are all nicked (stolen). They're only 'alf nicked. They come in at 'Arrod's near where I live last Firsday in de mornin' at de front, and aht to me at midnight at de back. If yer single, they'll get yer married; if yer divorced, they'll get yer married again; and, if yer married, they'll get yer ol' man (husband) chasin' yer rahnd de bedroom . . .'. It was a good example of Cockney talk and wit.

Sociology and pronunciation

Some apparently small differences of vowel sounds seem attributable to social class. Matthews suggests that, in words like 'now', the Cockney *nah* and *ne-u* represent different social dialects. The higher-class one is the diphthongal *ne-u*, since its *e-u* sounds more like the Standard English equivalent *ow* which is also a diphthong.

Rather similar is how the Cockney vowel in words like 'make' and 'wait' is judged. The 'true Cockney' utters something approaching *mike* and *white*; the slightly more refined has *meyk* and *weyt*; whilst one of high social class uses *make* and *wait* in line with Standard English.

The recent spread of London and its dialect

Cities are centres of administration and entertainment. This results in many different accents or local dialects meeting there. City dialects are therefore a mixture of modified standard language and, amongst other things, the dialects of surrounding rural areas. This is so in London.

City dialect spreads because younger people look to the city for entertainment, people go there to shop, and schoolchildren have to attend secondary schools on city outskirts because there are none in nearby small rural villages. Again all this applies to London.

London has become the most complex and spread-out city in the world and, just as it has spread geographically, so has its dialect. Shortly after the Great War the Becontree housing estate was built at Dagenham in Essex. It was the largest housing estate in the world. Its people, mostly East Londoners, did not adapt properly to their new surroundings, but kept their old way of life with its Cockney speech. Now Dagenham is just another area in the vast London conurbation. As good roads were extended and tube stations were created, suburban housing developments appeared beside them. (Houses near the Great West Road and the Kingston by-pass illustrate the former type, Morden and Cockfosters typify the latter.)

In 1923 dialect of the London type had spread northwards along the Stort Valley in north-west Essex along districts near main railway lines and main roads. It was also reaching other parts of the Home Counties (Hertfordshire, Surrey, Berkshire, etc.). In the 1939–45 War refugees left inner London, which was being badly bombed, for what was then the outlying countryside, never to return, and they took their Cockney dialect with them.

Since then, popular London speech has been extending as far as Folkestone and Brighton to the south and towards Norwich in the North, again along lines of easy road and rail communication. To the south-east the A2 road out towards Dover has also been extending the Cockney-type area, although not far away the A20 to Maidstone still runs through an area of quite different Kentish Weald dialect. And still the general drift to the Greater London area goes on, because fewer and fewer people are needed to work on farms and in rural industries. The railway and car have made it possible for millions more people to live out towards the country and yet work well inside London, so developing their modern London speech.

Parallel to the enormous expansion of outlying metropolitan boroughs has been a dramatic contraction of population in some of the inner areas. Whereas between 1921 and 1961 Hendon expanded from 58,000 people to 150,000, and Bexley's population rose from 21,000 to 90,000, other boroughs were losing residents. The greatest losses of population were in *Westminister* (as Cockneys sometimes by accident call it), *Saaf 'Ackney* 'South Hackney', *Ba'ersea* 'Battersea' and *Befnal (Bethnal) Green*, all in the heart of London.

To the inner areas has come a vast immigrant population. In the period 1973–78, in Hackney, Brent, Ealing, Haringay and Newham more than one baby born in every three was coloured, Brent holding the record with 42 per cent. Formerly North Londoners could nearly all be called Cockneys. Now many are from the Caribbean, saris and turbans can be seen alongside Western dress in the shops; and places like Palmer's Green, Stamford Hill in North Hackney, and Turnpike Lane north-east of it have large immigrant communities. All this immigration has not swamped Cockney – the change has rather been the opposite, with

Cockney sounds and words escaping from unlikely mouths; but it does mean that a very unusual un-English type of Cockney, often with quite different stress and intonational patterns according to the nationalities speaking it, has appeared in some areas. And, of course, some new expressions from abroad have appeared. *Man* 'friend' as in 'Gee, man, that's fine' is becoming common enough but we cannot yet call it Cockney. 'A ticket to Tottenham Court Road' may look correct in print, but when said in machine-gun fashion, very rapidly with each syllable given almost equal stress, is decidedly un-English and un-Cockney. In short, as each new immigrant arrives in London, another foreign language element bombards Cockney, but so far without great success.

Social conditions and customs

East End life was harsh. Its language confirms this, with many words for 'exhausted', 'slatternly', etc., along with many names for ordinary things like parts of the body and ordinary food and clothing, but very few for philosophic ideas, which only the leisured classes have time to ponder. Of someone in Tottenham, Edmonton or round Edgware Road, these Cockneys would say, ''E's well-awf', though the wealth was only comparative and obtained, perhaps, from a regular job and not drinking. The picture emerges of the Cockney community caught in a poverty trap, leaving little time for anything except work or sleep.

Poverty struck hard. In Bishopsgate they used to line up for yesterday's bread and round the dairy for cracked eggs. An informant's uncle used to pick up cabbage leaves dropped near Spitalfields fruit market to sell them, for 'If yer 'ad noffink, yer got noffink'. The father of another helper broke his wrist and split an arm muscle for 7s 6d, taking on all comers at a boxing-booth. Some people had to take off their dirty clothes before they went to bed to have them washed, and put them on again next morning because they were the only *togs* (clothes) they had. The poor were really poor, but they were hard workers.

There were strange recreational and other customs. In the early 1930s, for sixpence at the Troxy cinema on Commercial Road you could, after pushing for entry, see a short *fillam*, a *comic* (cartoon), three items of a stage talent-competition and then the main film; but, if the *dolly mixtures* (pictures) at some places were no good, the audience would roll winkle shells about the floor. Up Tib Street second-hand clothing was sold *awf of de floor* 'from the ground', laid out on a tarpaulin instead of a stall. Buying from that market was called *goin' rahnd the ol' gels*, though a few of the vendors were *fellers*. Off Cable Street in King David Lane a sergeant would emerge from the *cop-shop* (police-station) with his *coppers* in line behind him, to send them in turn away on their beats radiating from that lane. The lane's other special building belonged to the *Sally Army*, which did marvellous work providing East Enders with cheap *nosh*. Food would sometimes be *'lahanced aht* (allowanced out, rationed) in families, with a certain amount of bread per meal.

In the 'hungry 30s', when school dinners used to be 4d, Empire Day was made into a great occasion. Small Union Jacks were taken to school, normal lessons were abandoned, and the children were subjected to talks about India, Canada, *Sahf Africa* and other far-flung places. Just before noon the whole school might assemble, beating time with the flags, to voice the stirring march:

> *What is the meaning of Empire Day?*
> *Why do the cannons roar?*
> *Why does the cry 'Gawd Save the King!'*
> *Echo from shore to shore?* – and so on.

Times have changed – try belting that out now at, say, the London School of Economics!

One Empire Day a knock came at the school door and the teacher, trying to use the incident, said it might be the king himself. It was the dad of one of my informants, come to pay 1s 8d for his *gel's* dinners for the week. She has never felt so humiliated, though the teacher tried to cover it up by saying he was a king to his family.

Up to about 1936 many working-class Londoners made good use of their leisure time by taking a working summer-holiday hop-picking in Kent. Whole families of *'oppers*, wheeling their belongings in a *barrer*, would converge on London Bridge and Woolwich stations to board special *'oppin'-trains*, leaving a relative to push back the empty *barrer*; or went in lorries (which for 2s 6d a head would also bring their relatives to see them at week-ends). A lot of East Enders used to enjoy it. Families in hop-picking areas would rise at 6 a.m. while the dew was still on the hops, and had a special hop-picking song:

They all say 'oppin's lazy.
I don' believe it's true.
We on'y go dahn 'oppin'
To earn a bob or two. . . .

As this Cockney book is not primarily a sociological survey, the section must conclude. But I often feel that the most important things found are not pronunciations, words or grammar, but the culture they portray. There lies another good reason for this chapter.

9
How to Study
Urban Dialect

This chapter is intended for students writing essays, dissertations or theses or preparing talks on the subject, and for the general reader with a normal person's interest in anything fascinating. The more you find out about city dialects, the more fascinating they become.

Why study dialect?

A chief reason for such study is to learn more about Standard English. It does not make a student into a straw-chewing country bumpkin or a most ignorant 'townee', for it teaches a great deal about acceptable English. This is because, when you analyse expressions like *cack-'anded*, *dusty* for a dustbin-man and *jumped awf of de pier*, you have to work out carefully the boundaries between dialect and the standard language. No wonder that throughout the educational world dialect study is coming more and more into fashion. It is respectable and worthwhile.

Work to a plan

For sound results your study must be systematic. For centuries many enthusiasts have collected dialect words in haphazard fashion, rejoicing to hear, for example, of a *mardy* for a spoilt child in Manchester or a *bosh* for a kitchen sink in the Forest of Dean. Such answers are of little scientific value unless the searcher also records who said it and when. For systematic ways of collecting rural dialect, he should consult the Introduction to the Leeds University *Survey of English Dialects*. For urban dialect-collecting the techniques are about to be shown.

Choice of city

Normally this will be dictated by matters of convenience. The obvious choice is the city in or near which you live, where you can easily understand the talk and where you may know many suitable people to listen to. It is also a very good plan, and not an expensive or time-consuming one, to compare the language of two nearby cities. A close examination will show remarkable differences even in the language of cities almost within sight of each other. For example, if you live conveniently near to them, try Liverpool and Manchester, Durham and Newcastle, Gloucester and Worcester, Worcester and Birmingham, or Leicester and Nottingham. You will find no two cities alike. A third general way is, when you are on holiday, to keep an interested ear for the local speech in, say, a city like London or Edinburgh, or a large resort like Blackpool or Brighton.

Background preparation

The more you know about British dialects in general, the better placed you will be to explore those of individual cities because, even if their language has not yet been studied in detail (and it rarely has), that of their surrounding areas will most certainly have been analysed both in academic books and local county glossaries. For this reason you are recommended to browse through any of the books mentioned in the Bibliography which you can obtain, borrow or look through in a local reference library. Then seek, in its local studies section or that of a local university library, other relevant language material.

Once in the chosen city, get hold of a city street-map from its main library or a local shop to show you places and distances. The library may well have other local dialect books which you have not consulted and tapes of local speakers. Such tapes, usually located in the local studies section, are at last becoming more available, though still too few cities have them. They are especially good for checking pronunciation and grammar.

Time needed

There is no doubt whatever that the best chances fall to a resident investigator with plenty of time. The shorter the visit, the greater the risk of inaccuracy. Flying visits have their uses to sample the problems and check results afterwards if need be. But to hurry the main investigation, even if aided by an excellent tape-recorder, is hardly a recipe for success.

The best plan is to start cautiously and speed up later, when good informants have been selected and friendly relations with them firmly established. This is not advice to be lazy. In the early stages you can work hard making contacts and seeing recommended informants, as only by talking to them face-to-face can you properly decide whether they fit your purpose. They too have to see that you are not trying to make fun of them, or cheat them, or are involved in a hopeless, ill-conceived mission. Time spent getting hold of the best speakers available will make the visits, for them and you, a real pleasure.

Transport

Travelling to a city is easy. It may be by train, bus, car, cycle, etc. or by a combination of methods. Trains are quicker (when there is a suitable line) but dear, buses cheaper but slower, cars convenient but expensive and awkward to park near city centres, cycles and mopeds very manoeuverable but open to exhaust fumes, weather and the dangers of heavier traffic. Each method has merits and de-merits.

In towns and cities some walking should not be scoffed at. Smaller ones can be quickly and fairly pleasantly crossed in this way. Even in London from my usual base near Waterloo, though naturally making good use of the *Oxo cube* and the *swear an' cuss* for more outlying districts, I did plenty of walking. The amount of foot-slogging has to be balanced against its claimed contribution to health, and the money and time available.

Accommodation

Special accommodation may not be necessary. You may live in or quite close to the chosen city; or feel that your survey can be accomplished by a day visit or a series of them. However, if you are working in a strange city, overnight stays help a great deal and are often essential, because they allow you so much longer on the spot.

Accommodation will of course vary, but as a general plan it is wise to seek the cheaper variety. Not only does it disturb your wallet less, but it tends to keep you more in touch with average residents. Indeed the staff of your temporary headquarters or your hosts themselves might prove good initial contacts or informants. A good way to locate cheap accommodation is to look in a holiday guide or the local evening paper. (Write for a copy to be posted to you if necessary.)

Sampling

The only accurate sample is 100 per cent. As a move towards this desirable end, the modern, including the American, practice is to interview large numbers and in as random a fashion as possible. Theoretically this is excellent, but it remains true that a well-experienced fieldworker can make a choice just as good as, or better than, that of the most intricate computer-based system. The reason is that, although scientific methods can give a print-out of an extremely average cross-section of the community, it is one thing to have their names but quite another to persuade each to be interviewed and to speak and go on speaking in a perfectly natural way.

A common method of sampling is to pore through electoral registers, taking, say, every hundredth name. As the population per city ward varies greatly, selection of the hoped-for sample can be weighted accordingly. Similarly it can be weighted for age, sex, occupation, race, religion, and so forth. But often there is a built-in bias. Fathers out at work will be more difficult to contact than housewives. Men in prison, youths in the armed forces, mothers in labour, the very aged ill in bed, and families holidaying in Malta will all be hard to talk to. A survey of what parents think of their children's speech will neglect the views of childless parents; and, if it starts from lists of pupils, may concentrate e.g. only on parents with children in the upper classes of primary school.

In sampling cities, you must choose between a wise personal sampling and trying to break down into numerous language compartments the talk of, say, half a million people. Under how many divisions should they be grouped – ten, a hundred, a thousand? It is claimed that the number of social groups in a population of a million is much the same as in one of 10,000; but, even if it is so, a fully mathematical sampling is a mammoth task well beyond the resources of the average researcher. You must use your discretion.

Directness of your survey

Another thorny problem is how directly the information should be gathered. Well-known methods include the following:
(a) *The postal questionnaire*, the method used for Joseph Wright's great *English Dialect Dictionary* of 1904, and in the 1950s for the initial stages of the University of Edinburgh's important survey of

Scottish dialects. Its merits are speed, comparative cheapness (even in these times of increased postal charges), and especially the great number of localities which can be covered. Its handicap is that of having to sift written explanations instead of using the wider possibilities of talking face-to-face.

(b) *Telephone enquiries.* Useful as a follow-up.

(c) *Fieldworker with a set questionnaire.* Disadvantages are the expense and the fact that special local features may escape the language net. The advantage is that the fieldworker gets to know his questions very well, so that the interviews often go like clockwork.

(d) *Fieldworker varying his questions from place to place*, naturally after suitable background preparation. This allows great elasticity of treatment and makes it technically possible to capture any well-known local expression.

There are much poorer ways. Collecting dialect terms from newspaper articles generally gives no exact clue to who uttered them. Taking samples from radio and television is highly intriguing, but one has to be most suspicious about how typical many of them are. Even the most dialectal person cannot in daily life go around being uproariously funny the whole time as many excellent modern comedians are on stage.

Even if, as strongly recommended, you rely chiefly upon your own investigations on the spot, another choice has to be made. The researcher 'on site' may collect dialect by a type of squatter's infiltration, just listening and asking few questions; or else by a 'blitz' attack through plenty of carefully framed questions to entice as many suitable answers as possible in a comparatively short time. In two spells as a docker, I was fortunate in being able to collect dock language almost surreptitiously. As a university fieldworker, I had the opposite experience of having to fire numerous carefully chosen questions and sub-questions at informants within the inside of a week in many villages up and down the country. Both methods can bring outstanding results, but circumstances usually dictate which to use. The squatter method is preferable, but you will probably find in practice that the usual way will be to rely on systematic questions.

Number of informants

This depends very much on the time at your disposal, but, the more informants you have, the safer the representative sample is supposed to be. It is sometimes quicker and better to talk to a work-gang or household together instead of to each member separately, for the members will stimulate each other; but in this case you must be extra-careful to note who is saying what. Do not rely on one person alone to represent an area, and certainly not a whole city, since we all have so many language registers and no two people's English is alike. The resultant cross-checking of one citizen's speech against another's is to compare varieties and sometimes to check the accuracy of your own note-taking.

Useful contacts

Joining one of the dialect societies (Lakeland, Lancashire or Yorkshire) can be a considerable help towards meeting people of similar interests. Links with a folklore association or a local history society are also extremely useful – it is surprising how close are the ties between local history and dialect.

The introduction

One regular procedure, both in Britain and abroad, is to send, along with a stamped addressed envelope or reply-paid card, a preliminary letter of introduction to intended informants to fix an interview time. It has, however, definite drawbacks, the chief being that informants are usually taken only from those who willingly reply. Equally a formal letter of introduction handed over at the door can easily put people off. Telephoning for an appointment is better but can give a few people time to make trivial excuses. Generally far the best is to make your own direct introduction, as a salesman would, by going to the door to explain your mission. If you are honest and cheery, showing yourself ready to return if you must at a more convenient time, you will very often succeed and into the bargain bring your helpers plenty of interest and enjoyment.

The 'go-between'

A far better way, however, than arriving on a stranger's doorstep out of the blue, is to have had the introductory spadework done for you by a knowledgeable local contact. Teachers and ministers of religion are particularly good here, whilst formal permission from the Social Services to visit old people's homes or day centres can be extremely useful. An introduction from anyone well-known to the informant will work wonders. It may appear a very slow start just to write to, 'phone or see your local contact, but the best final results are often achieved thus.

Unlike the letter of introduction direct to possible informants, there need be few misgivings about sending one to a local contact because, whether he (or she) is a local journalist, librarian, bank manager, shopkeeper or whatever, what you are seeking will be understood. Unlike the informants this contact need not of course be locally born and bred, so long as his knowledge, status, etc. are likely to put you from the start onto quite good terms with your helpers. By all means, therefore, make good use of any willing local contacts: they are worth their weights in gold, not only because of their knowledge but because mention of their names is so often the key to many doors and the utmost co-operation. The contacts themselves are usually most interested.

Choosing informants

Let us assume that you require helpers born and bred within the city. This is a more straightforward operation than taking a cross-section of those who happen to live there now, or who work in the city and in many cases commute to it. There is nothing theoretically against such an 'all-in' method but it is considerably more complicated.

Preferably start, therefore, by seeking 'natives': then later, if you wish to extend your survey to other residents, you will have a good basis for comparison. A word of warning, however, against using this word *native*. Its meaning has changed since the 1950s, when it was quite safe to tell a villager or townsman 'I'm looking for natives'. Nowadays, if you say that, you are likely to receive the answer, 'Oh, we've no problem with immigrants here'.

It is almost purposeless to stand at a street corner, look round the market or drop into the nearest pub in order to listen and question at random. Ideally you should obtain full background information about your speakers – name, address (partly in case of follow-up questions, either face-to-face, over the phone or by post), age, where born (even the city district may be significant), birthplaces of parents, education (start e.g. by asking for the name of your helper's last school and at what age it was left rather than tactlessly inquiring about examination results or lack of them) and how long he or she has spent in the city or that part of it. (Some of these details will have been provided by your contact, others can easily be obtained by incidental questions during your conversation.) Most speech habits are acquired during the years two to 20, so beware of those who in childhood or teens lived elsewhere in case they have assimilated 'foreign' terms.

Once your mission has been explained, you will find most people very co-operative, for it is a human characteristic to like doing the talking, even to a comparative stranger. It may be necessary to stress that you are conducting a scientific survey, and are not from the newspapers or the BBC, since, although many people love publicity, others hate it. You might also like to add that the results, if published in any way, to preserve confidentiality will just be recorded as from the city or a special district of it, and not with the helpers' names.

Informants should be intelligent, which is not necessarily the same as being book-learned. They should be reasonably alert: something may be gained from a long rambling account, but a shorter answer is preferable. Yet the object is not a series of one-word answers, for English is a living thing with its words strung together in sequence, not fossilised in separate cases as in a museum.

No very dogmatic rules can be adhered to about whom to choose, but those with speech defects should be excluded and those who speak dialect only for entertainment purposes, not also as their normal way of life. The hard-of-hearing labour under some handicap, and other things being equal those with normal hearing would be preferred. Blind people were once thought impossible for language-hunting purposes, as they could not see the objects under discussion; but the blind are often very intelligent indeed, sometimes with a vivid recollection of things seen before they suffered their handicap, and they have plenty of time. You must work from the situation as it unfolds.

Unless it is for a special purpose, try to resist the temptation to jot down answers without knowing their source. Sometimes I have taken students round large department stores to record unobtrusively speech coming from behind the counters. It can be good phonetic training but is unscholarly for an organised survey unless the birthplace and background of the shop assistants are known. Only recently, jammed inside a frenzied F.A. cup-tie crowd behind a goal-post, I was assailed by some remarkable language intended for the referee, but the particular spectators who caused it would have taken exception if they had thereupon been questioned about their life histories. There are limits even for the language enthusiast; and it would also be tactful to veil the name of the East End team concerned, which was playing abominably.

Time of interview

Choose times when your helpers are not too busy. Most elderly people like to get up late and potter around in the mornings: few like being questioned much before 11 a.m. Working people, and indeed most people, find the evening most convenient, though you cannot be everywhere at once. It may be possible to cater for these likes and dislikes by doing some 'office work' such as background reading, preparing questions, listening to tapes or checking results in the very early part of the day; reserving the rest of it, until late evening if possible, for interviews.

Length of interviews

They can be of any desired length from a few minutes to about two hours, for this has been proved about the limit of solid questioning that even the most willing people can comfortably endure. But such rigorous full-length questioning suits rather the old-fashioned questionnaire designed to elicit hundreds and hundreds of particular words. Much can usually be accomplished, if you have thought it out carefully, in about an hour.

By 'length' is meant length of the interview proper, after the preliminaries. Politeness has to be observed. If you were to start, 'I'm X, come to find out how you talk. Hurry up! Sit down, please . . .', you would be very rightly shown the door. Anything worthwhile takes time, but the length of interview is simply what you and your informant need, bearing in mind your other ports of call. Often, though, such interesting ideas will be exchanged that it will seem an absolute shame to tear yourself away.

Place of interview

Not vital. In cities you are at least safe from the extremes of weather and the worst absurdities of rural interviewing head-quarters (such as a foul-smelling piggery or a Devonshire ant-heap, which an older colleague and I once found ourselves using). I have collected urban language in streets, town halls, offices and factories; from 'holes in the road' and the upper reaches of skyscraper flats; from educational establishments, theatres and cinemas, cafés and clubs, betting shops, an indoor bowling green, and so on. Good informal ways of collecting background dialect are to hang around school or factory gates at *lousin'-time*, when the conversational rules differ markedly from those in polite homes or in church. Pub visits can produce very sound dialect, though one danger there is that many helpers, especially younger ones, believe you are looking chiefly for jokes and so provide a deliberately unreal and exaggerated sample of local language. Shops, bus-queues, markets and in fact anywhere where people habitually collect are other obvious places, but any language taken there – at least for scientific purposes – ought to be supported by background evidence about each speaker, which in such cases is not easily obtained. Undoubtedly for a neutral, calmly conducted, accurate survey the best places are your informants' own homes, where they feel comfortable and most at ease.

Types of questions

Questions may be taken from a well-known questionnaire like the Dieth-Orton one for the Leeds *Survey of English Dialects* using its more general questions of Books V to IX; or that with many diagrams used for the *Atlas Linguarum Europae* (Atlas of European Languages), for which about a hundred English localities have recently been investigated. Yet to fit your special aims it would be best to frame some or all of the questions yourself. To retain your helpers' interest, they are better grouped (into those about people, the house, the body, clothing, weather, etc.). Several types are possible:

1 Straightforward 'naming questions', such as 'What do you call this?' (pointing to it); or 'What do you call the narrow place going between houses?' to elicit answers like *alleyway*, *ginnel*, *snicket* or *twitchell*. Try to avoid in the question any word that might be a Standard English or dialect answer, to keep the question neutral. Even *passage* in the example just given might be dangerous, as it could be a genuine answer and hearing it from you might make the informant repeat it.

2 'Completing questions', where your interviewee finishes the sentence for you with his term e.g. 'The part of the house with comfortable armchairs where you would entertain visitors is

called . . .', which brings *parlour, sittin'-room, best room, lounge,* etc. The great bulk of questions should be of these first two types.

3 'Reverse questions' are occasionally needed, where the word is given and you simply ask for its meaning, e.g. 'What do you mean by a tea-cake (or *bonny* or *a moggy*)?'

4 A few 'talking questions' may be in order, where your helper is encouraged to give his or her views, e.g. 'Are the old words quickly dying?', 'Do people speak differently according to the area of the city where they were born?', 'Do you think that schools should pay more attention to speech?', 'When is rhyming slang used?'

Never fall back on bare translation; for, if you ask e.g. 'Do you call yours a toilet?', you are inviting the same answer, whereas the genuine one might be *lav, loo,* etc. At the very worst, you might be reduced to suggesting a choice, e.g. 'In some areas they call it a *netty, nessy* or *dunnikin.* Are any of those used round here?'

Initial approach

When knocking on people's doors, it is better to be quite open about your purpose. State that you are very interested in how different people talk in that area. At first it may be wise to avoid using the word *dialect*, though every urban area has one, as many people are ashamed of their dialect through the way they have been checked about it in society, at home and especially at school.

You must give reasons for language research which informants can understand and agree with. Good ones are: (1) the old language is fading, perhaps slowly, but needs catching before it goes; (2) you hope to compare the speech of different generations; (3) what you find will be useful in teaching, because even the best dictionaries and text-books are somewhat out-of-date before they are published, and this is the only accurate way to find out how language is developing.

If asked, explain that you are not from the newspapers or the BBC, since, though some speakers love the limelight, others would then shut up like a clam. It helps if you can find something in common – if you learn that you share a common interest or have been to the same place. It helps too if you ask about your informant's children. Show genuine interest (e.g. in their occupations or educational careers) because people's lives are highly interesting, and you will then be surprised how animated your informant suddenly becomes.

162 *How To Study Urban Dialect*

YOUR OWN ACCENT Talk in a casual manner. Speaking in an artificial Oxbridge accent is no aid, neither is trying to speak all the time like Cockneys or other citizens being investigated. If they know that you come from a different background, they will accept it. The only exception to this rule is where you deliberately copy a sentence they have given, trying to say it their way, but assuming the role of pupil with your helpers as teachers. This they love, and in such circumstances will patiently endure your questions and curious attempts to imitate local speech.

SCRIPT For general purposes, answers may be recorded in approximate spelling. Phonetic experts may not be too happy with these for more detailed scientific analysis; but, unless you happen to know phonetics, what else can be done? However, those who know or who can learn the symbols of the International Phonetic Alphabet, which is not too hard[66], will find it indispensable; whilst any shorthand writers can bring their particular ability into use. Whatever methods of transcription are employed, do not stop at one-word answers. Each is far more revealing in its full context, so take down on the left-hand side of the page the whole reply or most of it wherever possible. Moreover, as everyone unconsciously keeps moving from one speech plane to another, and as the most genuine expressions occur in free conversation, record on the right-hand side of the page the incidental material, i.e. detailed explanations and remarks about other things or to other people that are interspersed with the direct answers to your questions. If an answer comes after pressure, mark it appropriately with SW (for 'suggested the word') or SP ('suggested the pronunciation'). Note remarks like 'My mum often said that', 'That's rougher', 'That's posh', 'Kids say it mostly'.

TABOO WORDS For these, oral questioning is far better than writing letters. The voice may be lowered or the daring word weakened by laughter. People are often ready to say things they dare not write.

Grammar, word-stress and intonation

These are all very neglected fields of language investigation grammar probably because is is thought so complicated and stress and intonation supposedly for the opposite reason, that there i very little to say about them! These claims are doubtful, and al those aspects of language are quite important. Grammar, word stress and intonation are most easily collected from the incidental material, the stray remarks that pop out while main answers are being sought. Word stress and snatches of intonation can be written down on the spot, the former by stress marks (e.g. *'Rúnning for a 'bús*) and the latter by something resembling a music score, like this:

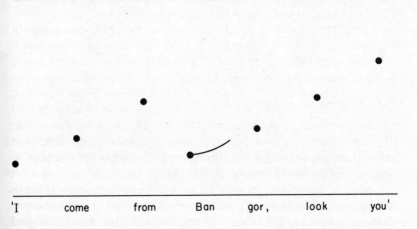

'I   come   from   Ban   gor,   look   you'

But the easiest way is to take along a tape-recorder and play back the passage later at your leisure.

Use of recording equipment

A tape-recorder is very handy for corroboration. Towards the conclusion of your visit one or more of your best informants, with the machine switched on, might be persuaded to talk about his life, the area, his family, local industries – in fact, anything. You are not there to do all the talking. Most inexperienced interviewers talk far too much. As well as short questions use pauses, nods and smiles to encourage further answers. This is especially useful in interviews that are being tape-recorded.

Be conversant with your machine. Make sure that it is correctly switched on and take care not to erase accidentally what has been recorded. Cut down extraneous noise by, if necessary, shutting windows against traffic hum, removing or stopping nearby ticking clocks, not scraping chair-legs, etc.

Before using a tape-recorder, tell your speaker frankly what you are going to do. Normally the best way is either to start the tape-recorder towards the end of the interview, when he is in full flow; or to have it running all the time, so that he eventually forgets all about it.

Use of pictures, diagrams, photographs, etc.

Pictures, diagrams and photographs can be a splendid help. Properly thought out, they can be great time-savers ('What's this? And this? Who's this?'). Tool-names, for instance, come easily by this method. Gestures are useful, e.g. to point to parts of the body and clothing. Demonstrations are another fine aid, e.g. to show walking pigeon-toed or splay-footed.

Don't be timid

Confidence in grasping interview chances will come with practice: most researchers are understandably rather shy at first, but informants themselves, by their pleasure at what you are trying to do, may help you to overcome any diffidence.

There is, however, another form of timidity of which quite a number of researchers are guilty. It is a reluctance to do little more than list answers. Theories, right or wrong, are interesting and often important – more important than the separate details on which they are based – so do please reach some conclusions from your survey into urban language. Even a negative conclusion, e.g. that the language is in such a mess that it cannot be adequately described or that it is in a state of continual flux is better than a mere list of certain words and pronunciations. Even though at first you see it only hazily, work towards some language goal.

Checking results

Results may be checked roughly on the bus or train going home, and more thoroughly as soon as possible afterwards. Check for word meanings in works like the O.E.D., *The English Dialect Dictionary*, and Partridge's slang dictionary (see Bibliography). Phoneticians will find the Leeds University *Survey of English Dialects* invaluable. If puzzles arise, contacts with informants may be re-established by letter, phone, or if convenient by another personal visit.

Historical analysis

It is possible to push the results of research farther back by noting etymologies – a surprising number of enthusiasts have such an interest – for which you should consult *The Oxford Dictionary of Etymologies* or other large standard dictionaries. From the big *Oxford English Dictionary*, the most famous in the world and available in its many volumes in reference libraries, you can obtain, next to the first quotation under any word, the date that word was first recorded in print. It should be realised, however, that all words must be current in the standard language for a while before there is time and opportunity to publish them in a dictionary. Therefore do not condemn a word as unacceptable in formal English just because it is absent from the first dictionary on which you lay hands. It may nevertheless be in the O.E.D. Supplement, or in a more recent work like the Penguin dictionary, or at the printer's ready to join a dictionary shortly.

Filing system

If the hobby grows on you, a filing system will be needed. Suitable for this are plain white cards of similar size, say about 5in. x 3in., roughly as thick as a postcard and obtainable cheaply from any jobbing printer. Write the head-word in the top right-hand corner of the card; and, if information is continued onto the back, mark the bottom right-hand corner of the front with a sloping line to remind you to turn over. Use intitials or symbols to indicate each speaker. Write fairly small and cross-reference where necessary. The use of different coloured inks for different speakers or different areas allows one card to show clearly the answers to a question from various sources. Transfer results from your answer sheets to these cards as soon as possible after the interviews, while details are vivid in your memory.

Keep trying

Like a good salesman you must persevere. It is sometimes said that there is no such thing as luck. Perhaps it would be truer to say that good luck balances the bad, or that you make your own luck, so that the best plan is to carry on regardless. In dialect work, as in everything else, perseverance pays. Good hunting!

10
Cockney's Future

Cockney used to have many more links with surrounding rural dialects. For example it had lost its *w* in 'woman' and gained an extra *y*- in *yearn* 'earn', both features which occur occasionally in southern dialects; along with *w* for *v*, which in 1890 Ellis noted for Essex. From such evidence it appears that Cockney has moved closer to Standard English than have its neighbouring rural dialects. Yet we cannot assume that Cockney will be quickly swallowed into Standard English. Some elderly Cockneys grumble that their type of speech is alive 'only in pockets', in small areas of inner London; but by this they mean that only there is it unaltered. Even where Cockney is altering it still survives, often quite strongly, throughout London.

How children speak is significant. Cockney schoolchildren use very dark *l*s, or actually vocalise them (as when they say that they walk up *hioos* 'hills' and drink school *miook* 'milk'). They are extremely fond of glottal stops (even though they do not know what they are), and their tongues slip unerringly round the special Cockney vowels. The fact that Cockney pronunciation is so strong in many youngsters argues solidly that it, and doubtless the special words that often accompany it, will have a lively active future, for Cockney schoolchildren are the adult speakers of tomorrow.

Cockney was exported from North and East London into early Australian speech when the first convicts arrived in Port Jackson in 1788, and about a century later A.J. Ellis[67] was stating that the Cockney form of speech was still prevalent in Australia. But, although many modern vowels of that country are reminiscent of Cockney, not all of them are; whilst nasalisation 'down under' seems to be growing and the glottal stop there is practically unknown. Australian speech is also in general less husky, drawled, and more levelly intoned. New Zealand talk also is not the exact equivalent of Cockney; and although Canada has its own delightful city of London (see Appendix A) no-one would imagine for a minute that its residents speak anything resembling Cockney. We cannot therefore truthfully say that Cockney lives on in the old British Empire.

Some writers are most pessimistic about Cockney's future. In the 1972 preface to his reprinted book, Matthews wrote sadly: 'I fear that the Cockney dialect will not long survive the common London music-hall, the costermonger's barrow and the street game. . . . The pub is not the social centre that it once was; street markets are fewer; slums have largely given way to isolating towers. Family gatherings are less frequent as members move into the outer suburbs. . . . And children stay longer at school . . . only now and then, among older people, market sellers, Covent Garden porters . . . and the like does one hear anything like the broad Cockney that was 30 years ago much more common'.

Most of this is very true, for Cockney is certainly under pressure. Americanisms are affecting it, although admittedly via the mass media. The music-hall, which did so much to foster it, has been replaced by the *telly* and many a small house-party by mass commercial bingo. Some of the older industries with their special terms are dead or dying. For instance, over a third of Port of London dockers are aged over 50, so that not only their special words like *greenacre* for a spill but even more general ones like *guv'nors* for their administrators and employers, may fairly soon disappear.

Furthermore, old Cockneys are much less isolated than the rural elderly. They have better transport, are gathered more efficiently by the social security system, and have had the opportunity of meeting a wide cross-section of people in city jobs. Cockneys who have *uplifted deirsells* 'improved their status' usually either do not want to admit their origin or may have a hazy notion about it, not realising, for example, that 50 years ago Edmonton where they were born was on the fringe of London. They will not easily admit to having come from *Black'eaf* or Woolwich, which are quite rough areas. Some of them imagine they have climbed out of one big hole into a smaller hole and then escaped altogether.

Yet countless thousands of London's citizens are still fiercely and proudly broad Cockney in speech, and when excited those with milder dialect drop right into a broader version. Many of the old words remain and much of the older slang; though many new words, including Americanisms and plenty of new slang, are altering the picture. Where the special Cockney vocabulary has largely gone, its pronunciation is much harder to eradicate and the special tag-questions like *ain't I?* and *weren't I?* are likely to persist.

Labov, the great American socio-linguist, seems to think that all social classes in speech may eventually disappear, but is this possible? It would be an intolerable world if every Londoner spoke exactly alike, with the same stock expressions, sounds and intonation. I have always found in London a more independent and (dare it be said?) more hopeful picture; whilst it must surely take an enormous stretch of imagination to think of London without a Cockney. Clearly the Cockney dialect is changing, and must develop with the changing times, but that does not mean that it will disappear.

A dialect continues to live so long as the community speaking it possesses a cohesiveness and sense of tradition. These Cockney has; and thus it appears that, although like all British city dialects Cockney will be further modified by Standard English, varieties of Cockney are here to stay.

Appendix A:
The Dialect
of Another London

In 1978 I had the good fortune to attend an international conference of dialectologists in another city of London, that in Western Ontario, Canada. This London, only 180 years old and originally a frontier post, has now a fine university which possibly one day will rival our London University, a Hyde Park, a suburb of Richmond, and areas named High Holborn and Highbury. It too stands on the River Thames; it has a Covent Garden, which has always been the name of its market; along with its own St Paul's Cathedral, Blackfriars Bridge, Pall Mall, Cheapside, Victoria, Chelsea Green, etc. Like all cities in 'Upper Canada', it has its King, Queen and Princess Streets; but no Strand, Buckingham Palace and surprisingly, since it is often called the 'Forest City', no Epping Forest. Presumably on a much smaller scale there must be a parallel in violence, for in Canada a knife attack on a shopkeeper took place one evening near me, just as a murder occurred off Whitechapel Road, Stepney, on one of the days I was investigating that area.

What stand out, despite surface similarities, are its differences. It is no capital, though conceivably it could be, situated as it is in the heart of the nation's cornbelt where perhaps your favourite breakfast cereal has come from. In general, Canadian Londoners are considerably more prosperous than their British counterparts. In pronunciation they are of course widely different, especially in heavy nasalisation and r-coloured vowels. Unlike Cockneys, most of them seem to dislike the very local speech of other parts of their county.

This second London has been, it is claimed, the home of more millionaires than any other part of Canada, so there is a hint for restless Cockneys. However, its language yields far less than the treasure trove of British London. After making relevant enquiries in homes, streets, markets, churches, and at a local baseball match where car roofs were damaged by balls struck outside the ground, I returned with information samples of which are set out below:

Cockney	Standard English meaning	London, W. Ontario
autumn	'autumn'	fall
break, 'levenses	'mid-morning snack'	brunch (also for a combination of breakfast and lunch)
drawt, dry spell, dry time	'drought'	draht
lights	'traffic lights'	stop lights
mates	'friends'	pals
pollywags	'tadpoles'	pollywogs
quarter-past-free feet	'splay-footed'	duck-footed
ring, circ-u	'ring round the moon'	hazy edge
splinter	'splinter'	slivver
tea	'evening meal'	supper (heaviest meal of the day)
tippeny-tawter, etc.	'see-saw'	titter-totter

Such sample comparisons shed light on interesting differences in language and culture between the two Londons. A look at South Africa's East London, which sounds from its name even closer to Cockney, might reveal more striking differences. Cockney has no serious rival.

Appendix B: Vowel Charts

Cockney vowels

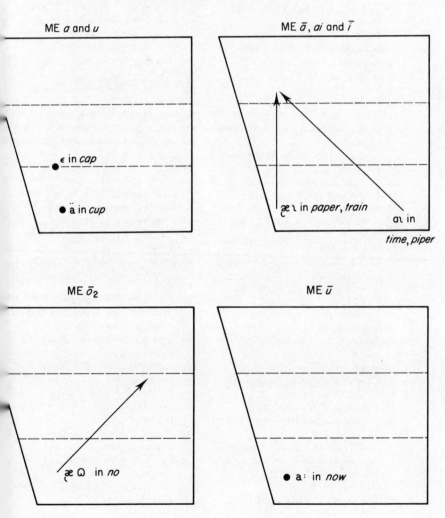

ME *a* and *u*

ε in *cap*

ä in *cup*

ME *ā*, *ai* and *ī*

æ˩ in *paper, train*

aɩ in

time, piper

ME *ō₂*

æᴑ in *no*

ME *ū*

aː in *now*

Notes

1 *English Dialects – their Sounds and Homes*, p. 57
2 *English Dialects – their Sounds and Homes*, p. 35
3 In *London's Dialect*, Priory Press, pp. 8–9
4 Wells, J.C., *Jamaican Pronunciation in London*
5 *Notes and Queries*, series II, vol. 22, pp. 349–50
6 Vol. I, pp. 39–40
7 In *History of English*, a BBC talk broadcast by Prof. H. Orton
8 C.M. Matthews, *English Surnames*, appendix 8
9 *London Labour and the London Poor*, pp. I, 24, 169
10 *Lore and Language*, vol. 2, no. 2
11 *Language of Dickens*, p. 72
12 Part II, p. 11
13 *Daily Telegraph*, 8 April 1896, p. 6, col. 1
14 *Macbeth*, III. 2. 45
15 Cf. American *brahma* for a variety of chicken taken in the nineteenth century from India
16 Page 112
17 23 March 1975
18 7 Nov. 1976
19 Brook, G.L., *Varieties of English*, p. 136
20 7 Sept. 1979
21 Cf. EDD *moggie* and Vigfusson
22 Cf. EDD *hoddy-doddy*
23 *Dictionary of Historical Slang*
24 Oxford English Dictionary *slang* sb.³ and *sling*, v¹.
25 Vol. I, pp. 217–8. His examples of it mentioned in this paragraph are from vol. I, pp. 15, 181, 184; and vol. II. p. 34
26 See page 27 (gipsy words)
27 From rhyming slang. See page 99
28 Vol. I, p. 418
29 *Dictionary of Rhyming Slang*, pp. 5ff
30 Vol. I, p. 418
31 She has written other Cockney poems. See her book of verses *Words – just Words*, first published by Norman Hidden in his *Workshop New Poetry*
32 Vol. I, p. 411
33 See *net* in *Dictionary of Historical Slang*
34 Vol. I, pp. 11, 23–4, 33, 41
35 Vol. I, p. 472
36 Guildhall Library pamphlet 7223 under *his-n*
37 Of the 250 commonest Anglo-Saxon verbs, about two-thirds now take *-ed*. Cf. J. Wright, *Old English Grammar*
38 Chapters 37, 44
39 G.L. Brook, *Language of Dickens*, p. 242
40 Professor R. McDavid, quoted in *The Wall Street Journal* of 30 June 1978
41 *Early English Pronunciation*, Part V
42 *English Dialects – their Sounds and Homes*, p. 57
43 *English Dialects – their Sounds and Homes*, p. 35
44 *English Dialects – their Sounds and Homes*, p. 58
45 *Discovering English Dialects*, p. 32
46 *English Dialects – their Sounds and Homes*, p. 58
47 *History of Modern Colloquial English*, p. 200
48 Cf. Matthews, *Cockney Past and Present*, p. 162
49 Wyld, *History of Modern Colloquial English*, p. 233

50 *Early English Pronunciation*, pp. 226–8
51 *English Dialects – their Sounds and Homes*, p. 51
52 Matthews, *Cockney Past and Present*, p. 165
53 Page 158
54 *History of Modern Colloquial English*, p. 230
55 *English Dialects – their Sounds and Homes*, p. 57
56 See Treble and Vallins, *A.B.C. of English Usage*
57 *History of Modern Colloquial English*, p. 299
58 'Errors of Pronunciation used frequently and chiefly by the inhabitants of London', Guildhall Library pamphlet no. 7223
59 *Notes and Queries*, series II, vol. 22, pp. 349–50
60 *Short History of English*, 3rd ed., 1927, para 282(3)
61 Guildhall Library pamphlet no. 7223, pub. 1817
62 *History of Modern Colloquial English*, p. 292
63 Canto IV, 11, 117–18
64 Pages 150–1
65 3 November 1978
66 Compare Daniel Jones, *Outline of English Phonetics*
67 *Early English Pronunciation*, Part V, 225

Select Bibliography

AYLWIN, Bob, *A Load of Cockney Cobblers* (London's rhyming slang interpreted), Johnston and Bacon, 1973

BOWYER, R., *Study of Social Accents in a South London Suburb* (Beckenham), Leeds University M.Phil. thesis, 1973

BROOK, G.L., *The Language of Dickens*, Deutsch, 1970; and *Varieties of English*, Macmillan, 1972

DASH, J., *Good Morning, Brothers!* Lawrence and Wishart, 1969

DODSON, M., and SACZEK, R., *Dictionary of Cockney Slang and Rhyming Slang*, Hedgehog Enterprises, 1972

ELLIS, A.J., *Early English Pronunciation, Part V* and its abridgement *English Dialects – Their Sounds and Homes*; Early English Text Society, 1890

'Errors of Pronunciation, and improper expressions, used . . . chiefly by the inhabitants of London' (anonymous), Guildhall Library pamphlet no. 7223, 1817

FRANKLYN, J., *Dictionary of Rhyming Slang*, Routledge, 2nd ed., 1961

HOTTEN, J.C., *Dictionary of Modern Slang, Cant and Vulgar Words, used at the present day in the streets of London*, J.C. Hotten, 1859

HOUSE, H., *The Dickens World*, O.U.P., 2nd ed., 1942

JACOBS, W.W., *The Nightwatchman and other Longshoremen*, Hodder and Stoughton, 1932

JONES, Jack (ed.), *Rhyming Cockney Slang*, Abson Wick, 1971

KIPLING, R., *Barrack-Room Ballads*, 1889–91, Methuen, 1973

LAWRENCE, J., *Rabbit and Pork: Rhyming Talk*, Hamish Hamilton Children's Books Ltd., 1975

LEITH, R., *Dialectology in London* (about speech in Stepney, Hoxton and Kilburn), Leeds University M.A. thesis, 1971

MACBRIDE, M., *London's Dialect: an ancient form of English Speech*, Priory Press, 1910

MACKENZIE, B.A., *Early London Dialect*, O.U.P., 1928 (deals with it in Middle English times)

MATTHEWS, W., *Cockney Past and Present*, Routledge, 1938

MAYHEW, H., *London Labour and the London Poor*, Cass, 1967

ORTON, H. et al., *Survey of English Dialects*, E.J. Arnold (Leeds), 1962–71

PARTRIDGE, E., *Dictionary of Slang and Unconventional English*,

5th ed., Routledge, 1961; and its abridgement *Dictionary of Historical Slang*, Routledge, 1973

ROSTEN, L., *Joys of Yiddish*, Penguin, 1971

SHAW, G.B., *Pygmalion*, 1920. Also *Captain Brassbound's Conversion*, 1899, particularly for his introduction to Act I and his dialect notes accompanying the play

SIVERTSEN, E., *Cockney Phonology*, Oslo University Press, Studies in English no.8, 1960

SPEIGHT, J., *Thoughts of Chairman Alf*, Robson's Books Ltd., 1973; and *It Stands to Reason* (autobiographical); Futura Publications, 1974

VICINUS, M.J., *Industrial Muse: a study of the 19th century British Working-Class Literature*, Croom Helm, 1975

WAKELYN, M.F., *English Dialects: an Introduction*, Athlone Press, 1972; and *Discovering English Dialects*, Shire Publications Ltd., 1976

WELLS, J.C., *Jamaican Pronunciation in London*, Oxford, Philological Soc.pub.no.25, 1973

WERTH, P.N., *The Dialect of Leytonstone*, Leeds University B.A. thesis, 1965

WRIGHT, J., *English Dialect Dictionary*, Oxford, 1904 (abbreviation EDD)

WRIGHT, P., *Language of British Industry*, Macmillan, 1974

WYLD, H.C., *Short History of English*, Murray, 3rd ed., 1927; and *History of Modern Colloquial English*, Blackwell, 3rd ed., 1936

Index

glottal stops 23, 136–7
Gloucester Rd 141
'go-between' for dialect research 156–7
Golden Lane estate 11
gorse, words for 79
grammar 101, 114–25, 162
Great West Rd 146
greenacre 86–7, 167
Greenwood, J. 17
greetings 46–8, 112
Grimald, N. 49
groin, a ring 62
Gunners, Arsenal 51
guv'nors 70, 167
gypsies, words for 32

h- initially 134
Hackney 8, 11, 134, 144, 147
Hainult 12
hair, words for 37, 105
ham, meaning of 65
Hammersmith 141
Hampstead Heath 105, 143
Haringay 147
Harmondsworth (Middlesex) dialect 8
Harrods' 145
head, words for 36, 90, 105
Hebrew 39–41
helpers for dialect 155
Hendon 147
Henry IV 14
Hertfordshire dialect 13, 126, 147
Higgins, Prof. 145
Highgate language 143
Hindustani words 25
historical analysis 164
Hoccleve 13
homosexuals 34
hop-picking 149; song 150
Hotten, J. C. 104
house terms 66–9; slang 92
Hoxton 132
Hoy, Barbara 108
Huntingdonshire immigrants 13
Hyde Park 136, 142
hyper-correction 116
Hypocrite 122

idler 70
imitating accents 162
immigrants' language 42–6, 140, 147–8
imperfect rhyming slang 99
impossible object, terms for 70

in course 15
incidental material 162
indefinite pronouns 117
indigestion, verbal 95
informants 155
-ing verbal forms 121
Inland Revenue 30
Inner Circle railway 141
inquisitive, words for 37
insects 80
intensifiers 123
interjections 124–5
International Phonetic Association 126, 162
interviewing methods 151–65
intonation 140–1, 148
  of immigrants 43–4
  recording of 162–3
introductions to dialect speakers 156
'intrusive r' 135–6
Irishisms, London type 55
Isle of Dogs 63, 74
Islington 11, 143
Italian words 25

Jacobs, W.W. 17–19
Jamaican immigrants 45, 140
jargon of markets 58–60
Jews 39–42
Jo, Dickens's crossing-sweeper 15
Johnson, Samuel 49
jokes against apprentices 70
Jones, surname 30
Julius Caesar 14

*k*s weakly exploded 136
Kaukneigh Awlmineck 129
Kentish 8, 12, 126
Kentish Weald dialect 147
Kew Gardens, go to 50
kind of 57
King's College 131
King's Cross 141
Kingston by-pass 146–7
Kipps 17
kitchen 68
Knight of the Burning Pestle 13

l 134
Labov 168
ladies urging clear speech 136–7
Lakeland Dialect Society 156
Lambeth 11

Standard English 13, 19, 45
steal, words for 70, 88
Stepney 11, 49, 66, 134, 169
Stoke Newington 72, 81
Stort Valley 147
story-telling techniques 120, 122
stranger, terms for 46
street, disappearing word 76
street-sellers' language 12, 16, 119, 145–6
stress 114–6, 121, 148
    in immigrant speech 43
    in rhyming slang 98
strong language 52, 144
strong verbs 118–9
Struth! 53
study of urban dialect 151–65
subjunctive 121
Sunday Express 52
surnames, of London 29–30
Surrey, dialect 8, 126, 145, 147; surnames 29
Survey of English Dialects 7, 151, 164
swearing 51–4, 123, 144
Sweet, H. 19
syllable lost 139

t, becoming *r* 139; loss of 139; of Indians and Pakistanis 43; weakly exploded 136
taboo words 162
tag-questions 44, 120–1, 168
tape-recordings 152, 163
Taylor, surname 30
teachers as contacts 156; urging clear speech 136–7
technical words 25, 29–30, 69–74
teem (of rain) 50, 79
teeth, words for 105
telephone inquiries 155
th becoming *f*, *v*, *d* 137
Thackeray 14, 137
Thames, River 8
than 123
the 9
    with illnesses 121
The 'Ouses in Between 22
theatrical rhyming slang 95
thieves' slang 88, 94–6, 111
Thieving Lane 30
Till Death us do Part 23
time, of day 83; of interview 159; enough for dialect survey 152–3
train nicknames 73

transcriptions of dialect 162
transport to dialect area 153
Tristran da Cunha dialect 137
toak 63–4
toby(man) 60
Toc H 8, 31
toilet, words for 68, 77
tongue-top, movements 127–8
Tottenham 11, 148
Tottenham Court Rd 43
totters 22, 32, 90–1
Tower of London 58
tube-station names 141
tube-stationmen's language 141
Tuer, A.W. 17, 141
TV, influence 13, 95, 143, 155; rhyming slang 95, 109

um 57
understatements 78–9, 118
underworld rhyming slang 102
union abbreviations 82
unknown name 62
untidy (person) 33, 67
unstressed vowels 133–4
untruthful 37
unwell, feel 57
urban dialect study 151–65

v, for *th* 23, 137; interchanging with *w* 137–8
value judgments about Cockney 142–3
vehicle terms 62–3
verbs 118–21
Victoria 141
Viking words 25
violence in cities 169
visitors baffled by Cockney 141
'vocalised' *l* 127, 134
vowels, definition 127; diagrams 128, 171
vulgar language 51–4, 107

w, confused with *v* 14–15, 17, 137–8; for *r* 135
Wakelin, M. 127
Walker, J. 115, 135
Walton-on-the-Hill (Surrey) dialect 8
Walworth 8
Wapping 11, 28
Wardour St English 48
was not 120
washing-day words 68–9
Waters, Elsie and Doris 20

Index